Load Balancing with HAProxy

Open-source technology for better scalability, redundancy and availability in your IT infrastructure

About the Author

Nick Ramirez is a software developer living in Columbus, Ohio. He is currently helping companies improve through the use of DevOps, automation and infrastructure-as-code. He lives with his wife and two cats and can often be found exploring National Parks, plugging wires into breadboards, and learning how to program Arduino.

Twitter @NickMRamirez

Credits

Cover Art Mohamedmusthafa, www.fiverr.com/mohamedmusthafa

Technical Reviewer Chris Ramirez

Copyright 2016 by Nick Ramirez

All rights reserved. This book or any portion thereof may not be reproduced or used in any manner whatsoever without the express written permission of the author except for the use of brief quotations in a book review.

Chapter 1

Hello, HAProxy

In this book, we're going to tackle learning HAProxy, which is an open-source load balancer that you can download and install for free and quickly start splitting requests for your website or other TCP-based services among many backend servers. The benefits of learning about HAProxy are astounding, especially as we think about adapting to the demands of the modern Web where 24/7 uptime is expected and websites must be able to handle large waves of traffic.

HAProxy listens for incoming requests and then forwards them to one of your servers. As demand grows, you can add more servers to handle it. The client never needs to know about the extra machines or change the way that they access your service. Instead, HAProxy makes the entire cluster look like one, very powerful server.

When your website or service is backed by a group of machines, you'll be able to handle much more traffic. You'll get better performance because load will be spread over a number of nodes and you'll be able to upgrade software, deploy websites or swap out servers without interrupting service. Probably the best advantage to using HAProxy is that a hardware failure that takes down one of your machines will no longer take your website down with it. With that, let's get started!

In this chapter, we'll cover the following topics:

- What HAProxy is
- The history of the project
- Who uses it

- How it works
- The benefits of using it
- The platforms it can be installed on
- What it costs
- Things it is not meant to do

What is HAProxy?

HAProxy is a software package that acts as both a reverse proxy and a load balancer for TCP-connected applications. When I say TCP-connected applications, I mean any application that uses the TCP protocol to transmit information between a client and a server. So then what is a reverse proxy? What's a load balancer? What are the benefits of using them?

A reverse proxy sits in front of your server and accepts requests from clients on its behalf. Think of it like a virtual ambassador for your server. Anyone from the outside world, the Web, will only be able to talk to the proxy. Then the proxy relays the message to your server, gets the response from it, and sends it back to the person who requested it. The original client never speaks directly to your server. The benefit of this is better anonymity and security, you can offload some work like compression to the proxy, and because we have this middleman your servers can be upgraded, moved or replaced without upending anything so long as the proxy can point to something else in the meantime.

Given you have more than one server, a load balancer will split incoming requests among them. It keeps track of which server got the last request and which one should get the next. To lean on an overused metaphor, it's the traffic cop of your network, making sure that all driving lanes, or servers in this case, are utilized equally. At the same time, the load balancer keeps track of which client connected to which server so the response is sent to the right person.

HAProxy is a reverse proxy and a load balancer. It sits between clients and your servers, proxying requests and load balancing the work so that no one server has to handle it all. Although HAProxy can direct traffic to many backend machines, from the client's perspective, it looks like they are communicating with only one. HAProxy is completely invisible to them. As we'll see, HAProxy is a powerful, modern-age software package with the potential to handle hundreds of thousands of simultaneous connections. It has features that allow it to work especially well with Web traffic, such as its ability to inspect and direct clients based on their HTTP messages.

What is the history of the project?

HAProxy has been around since 2002. It was created by Willy Tarreau, who also helps maintain the Linux kernel. It has had several major releases, is actively maintained and has ongoing development of new features. With the rise of microservices and more awareness of the benefits of a distributed architecture, it has become much more popular. From the beginning its aim has been to be fast, reliable and simple. The current stable release at the time of this writing is version 1.6, which is the version that we'll be covering. Development of version 1.7 in the works. You can keep up with the latest changes at http://www.haproxy.org/news.html.

Who uses it?

One of the nice things about HAProxy is that it's virtually impossible to tell who's using it. Although it sits in front of your Web servers, databases or other services, it doesn't run on any specific port or broadcast that it's there in other ways, such as by appending HTTP headers. However, we do know of some high-profile companies that have used it because they've blogged about it. The list contains quite a few companies that must handle large amounts of traffic, including Twitter, Instagram, Reddit, Github, StackOverflow and Alibaba.

How does it work?

HAProxy uses a single-threaded, event-driven architecture to receive requests from clients and dispatch them quickly to backend servers. It does not open a thread and wait for a server to respond. Instead, it moves on to do other work and returns when it receives a callback. This allows it to scale to many thousands of concurrent connections.

In contrast, Web servers like Apache and IIS dedicate a thread to each request and must keep that thread alive for the entire duration of the client-server session.

Because there's only a small number of threads that a computer can manage well, maybe a few hundred at most, Web servers are vulnerable to maxing out their resources whenever there's a spike in traffic. You'll typically see this as a spike in CPU since the computer is being asked to do more multitasking.

HAProxy is able to protect our servers by spreading the work evenly among them. When we start to get more traffic, we can simply add more machines, which gives us more resources to work with. This is the heart and soul of distributed computing. The term often used when describing adding more computers to share the load is horizontal scaling or scaling out.

What are some of its benefits?

HAProxy primarily gives us three things: better performance, better availability and better redundancy. When talking about measuring performance, we could think of it in terms of how fast our servers respond to clients. A Web server responds faster when it's not trying to do too much at the same time. Trying to respond to 100 simultaneous requests is going to cause the computer to divide its time among that many tasks. Things get tougher for the server when it generates its responses by using a programming language like Java or ASP.NET, which consume precious, shared CPU resources. The number of requests and the complexity in responding to them lengthens the time it takes to finish any particular task. When HAProxy distributes traffic equally to our servers so that no single machine is overloaded, response times get much faster.

Availability refers to whether a client is able to reach our services when they want to. If our server uses up all of its available threads, connection slots or CPU power, it won't be able to respond to more requests in a timely manner. It may even flat out reject some requests. Slowness is a form of unavailability because it means a client isn't able to get a response exactly when they want it. By distributing the work among many servers, HAProxy makes it more likely that there will be a server that's ready to perform the task.

Redundancy refers to having a backup plan for when things go wrong. If we only had one Web server and that server failed, we'd be out of luck! When we have multiple servers all doing the same job, if one crashes we'll have a spare or two to take over. We won't have to worry about losing service just because we lost one machine. HAProxy performs the vital role of clustering our servers together, or, in other words, grouping them into a pool of resources. Without it, a failed server would mean updating DNS or changing IP routing so that a new server could be swapped into its place. However, that strategy is slow and sure to cause an outage for at least some duration. When a server fails, HAProxy simply removes it from the cluster and traffic continues flowing to the other, available machines.

HAProxy gives us a lot of other features too including its ability to route traffic based on HTTP headers, cookies and URLs. We can have it do SSL termination, gzip responses, and even deny attackers. A big advantage is its ability to send health checks to our servers. This lets it know when a server has become unreachable. At that point, it stops forwarding traffic to it until it comes back online. These and other features add up to make HAProxy an invaluable component in your network infrastructure.

What platforms can it run on?

HAProxy can be installed onto Linux 2.4 and newer operating systems including Ubuntu, Debian and CentOS. It can also be installed onto Solaris, FreeBSD and AIX systems. At this time, there is no install package for Windows. However, although HAProxy itself can't be installed on Windows, it can still proxy traffic to and load balance Windows servers. We just need a Linux box in our network to host it.

What does it cost?

There is no charge for using HAProxy. It's free and open-source. It's distributed with the GNU General Public License, which means that you are able to use it without any fees in pretty much any way that you like.

Things get a little more technical if you want to make changes to the HAProxy source code in order to distribute propietary software based off of it. For example, if we make changes to the original code and want to distribute it, we'll need to do so under the GNU GPL license. That means that we must make the new code available for free to everyone.

However, things are different if we want to make a library that extends the functionality of HAProxy without changing its source code. The HAProxy C header files are distributed under the GNU Lesser General Public License. This means that our library can extend HAProxy by dynamically linking to it and our software can remain proprietary and closed-source.

Things it is not

We should keep in mind that there are some things that HAProxy can't do. For one, it is not a cache. It won't store HTML pages, images, or similar resources so that it can deliver them later without having to fetch them from an upstream Web server. Other tools like Varnish do pretty well at this and have features that fit that purpose.

HAProxy is also not a Web server in the way that IIS, Apache and NGINX are. It doesn't generate Web pages or respond to requests using Web frameworks like Ruby on Rails or ASP.NET. It will, however, forward requests to the appropriate Web servers and relay their responses. HAProxy's biggest value comes in its ability to provide scalability and high availability for your servers.

HAProxy is not a firewall. It can protect your servers from some threats like clients requesting too much data all at once. However, it is not designed to filter traffic between networks, detect and stop sophisticated attacks like cross-site scripting, or grant access to ports. There are other tools, such as ModSecurity and SonicWall, that act as that kind of security barrier. HAProxy works well alongside these tools.

Finally, HAProxy is not a forward proxy, like Squid is, that's used to hide your identity on the Web or to block employees from accessing certain websites. A forward proxy sits closer to the client, forwarding their requests to the Internet. HAProxy is a reverse proxy, which relays traffic for servers.

Summary

In this chapter, we covered a high-level overview of the features and benefits of using HAProxy. HAProxy acts as a reverse proxy and a load balancer. It has had a long history with ongoing development and is used by some high profile, heavily-trafficked websites.

HAProxy gives us better performance, availability and redundancy because it spreads work among many backend servers. This reduces the load on any one machine and gives us the flexibility to do maintenance without disrupting service.

HAProxy offers quite a few other features, but one of the most important is its ability to send health checks to our servers, removing them from load balancing when it sees a problem.

Although HAProxy performs some helpful functions, it doesn't do it all. It's not a cache, web server, firewall or forward proxy. It is, however, very good at what it aims to do. In the next few chapters, we'll jump into getting HAProxy installed and set up some basic configurations.

Chapter 2

Installing HAProxy

HAProxy can be installed on a variety of *nix operating systems. In most cases, there is a package available that will install everything we need to get up and running, but to get the latest version we may have to compile the source code ourselves. This isn't as bad as it sounds though, and is a good skill to have if you intend to turn on certain non-default features like geolocation.

In this chapter, we'll cover the following topics:

- Using Vagrant to create a virtual machine
- Installing on Ubuntu
- Installing on Debian
- Installing on CentOS
- Installing with Docker

Creating virtual machines with Vagrant

When you're just trying things out, you don't want to get bogged down in the chores of downloading an operating system, installing it into a hypervisor like VMWare or VirtualBox, and then configuring it for SSH. You just want to say: Give me a VM running Ubuntu! and sit back and watch it happen. That's where Vagrant comes in.

CHAPTER 2. INSTALLING HAPROXY

Vagrant is a command-line tool that creates virtual machines from public VM images that it downloads from its online repository. Vagrant works with existing hypervisors, like VirtualBox, to automate the creation and setup of a virtual environment on your personal computer. A lot of information can be found at https://www.vagrantup.com/docs, but I'll outline the basic steps involved.

First, download and install VirtualBox and then Vagrant:

- VirtualBox - https://www.virtualbox.org/wiki/Downloads
- Vagrant - https://www.vagrantup.com/downloads.html

Then browse the Hashicorp Vagrant repository.

- Hashicorp Repository - https://atlas.hashicorp.com/boxes/search

You'll find many publicly available virtual machine images there. For example, the boxcutter/ubuntu1604 image installs Ubuntu 16.04, codename Xenial Xerus. Copy the name of the image and then open a command prompt. Create a new directory, navigate into it, and then call the **vagrant init** command with the name of the image you'd like to use. The following commands will work on Windows or Linux:

```
~$ mkdir ubuntu_project
~$ cd ubuntu_project
~$ vagrant init boxcutter/ubuntu1604
```

You should see a message like this:

> A `Vagrantfile` has been placed in this directory. You are now ready to `vagrant up` your first virtual environment! Please read the comments in the Vagrantfile as well as documentation on `vagrantup.com` for more information on using Vagrant.

The **vagrant init** command generates a file called Vagrantfile in the current directory. It mostly includes helpful comments for getting started. The essential line that configures which image to pull from the Hashicorp repository is **config.vm.box**. It will look like the following:

CHAPTER 2. INSTALLING HAPROXY

```
config.vm.box = "boxcutter/ubuntu1604"
```

Before we create our VM, let's put it into a network so that we can give it its own IP address.

You may want to create a virtual private network that you can use to access your virtual machine. This kind of network will only be visible on your computer and makes it possible to assign a unique IP address to your VM, rather than access it as localhost. Update your Vagrantfile so that it contains the `config.vm.network` setting. An updated Vagrantfile will look like this:

```
# -*- mode: ruby -*-
# vi: set ft=ruby :

Vagrant.configure(2) do |config|
  config.vm.box = "boxcutter/ubuntu1604"
  config.vm.network "private_network", ip: "192.168.50.10"
end
```

You're free to use any private IP address. If, later on, you create more virtual machines, they'll be able to communicate with one another over the private virtual network as long as they are all assigned IP addresses within the same subnet. For example, any IPs between 192.168.0.0 and 192.168.255.255 would be in the same subnet. Next, let's create our VM. Call `vagrant up`.

```
~$ vagrant up
```

Vagrant will download the image and install it by using VirtualBox. When it's ready, you'll be able to SSH into it as the user vagrant with a password of vagrant. Those are the defaults, so calling `vagrant ssh` should log you in without needing any more information.

```
~$ vagrant ssh
```

Note that if you're doing this on a Windows host, which doesn't come with SSH, you can install Git for Windows to get all the Linux-y tools on Windows including the `ssh` command. It's available at https://git-scm.com/download/win. During the installation, be sure to select the option to add the Unix tools to your Windows PATH environment variable.

If you run a Web server on this VM, you'll be able to access it through the virtual private network. Simply type http://192.168.50.10 into your browser's address bar. This makes setting up a test environment quick and easy. You can even define several virtual machines within the same Vagrantfile. For example, to create two Ubuntu machines, one to host a Web server and another to host HAProxy, we can use the `config.vm.define` setting to define a block of settings for each machine. They will be able to communicate with one another over the network.

```
# -*- mode: ruby -*-
# vi: set ft=ruby :

Vagrant.configure(2) do |config|
  config.vm.define "webserver" do |machine|
    machine.vm.box = "boxcutter/ubuntu1604"
    machine.vm.network "private_network", ip: "192.168.50.10"
  end

  config.vm.define "haproxy" do |machine|
    machine.vm.box = "boxcutter/ubuntu1604"
    machine.vm.network "private_network", ip: "192.168.50.11"
  end
end
```

Then call `vagrant up` to create both machines:

```
~$ vagrant up
```

When you're finished using your VMs, you can either stop them with the `vagrant halt` command or throw them away with the `vagrant destroy` command.

Installing on Ubuntu

On Ubuntu 16.04 Xenial Xerus, use the apt package manager to install HAProxy 1.6. Start by installing the software-properties-common package:

CHAPTER 2. INSTALLING HAPROXY

```
~$ sudo apt install software-properties-common -y
```

Next, reference the HAProxy repository, ppa:vbernat/haproxy-1.6.

```
~$ sudo add-apt-repository ppa:vbernat/haproxy-1.6
```

Next, update Ubuntu's package list.

```
~$ sudo apt update
```

After this completes, install the haproxy package.

```
~$ sudo apt install haproxy -y
```

Now you should be able to check that HAProxy was installed with the following command:

```
~$ haproxy -v
```

You can also verify that the HAProxy service is running.

```
~$ sudo service haproxy status
```

You should see output like the following:

```
haproxy.service - HAProxy Load Balancer
Loaded: loaded (/lib/systemd/system/haproxy.service; enabled;
  vendor preset: enabled)
Active: active (running) since Tue 2016-03-01 03:10:49 UTC; 31min ago
```

You'll also find new files in the following locations:

Directory	What it's for
/usr/sbin	Contains the haproxy program.

Directory	What it's for
/usr/share/lintian/overrides	Lintian is a Debian package checker. The file here overrides rules that would otherwise cause the HAProxy package to be flagged as having an error.
/usr/share/doc/haproxy	Documentation for HAproxy that can be viewed with `less` or `vi`.
/run/haproxy	Contains a UNIX socket that HAProxy binds to during startup.
/var/lib/haproxy	Contains data that HAProxy stores while running.
/etc/logrotate.d/haproxy	Configures HAProxy to use logrotate, which manages how logs are compressed and rotated.
/etc/default/haproxy	Contains a defaults file for HAProxy that can override aspects of how the service starts up, such as where to look for its configuration file.
/etc/haproxy	Contains the HAProxy configuration file and a directory where HTTP error pages are defined.
/etc/init.d	Contains the initialization script for the HAProxy service.

Throughout the book, we will be changing the configuration file located at /etc/haproxy/haproxy.cfg. This file can be edited in just about any text editor. If you're using Vagrant, then a directory will have been created at /vagrant that links to your host machine. So, you could edit the file there, then access it on your VM from this directory. Just be sure to restart the service afterwards by calling `sudo service haproxy restart`.

Installing on Debian

On Debian 8 Jessie, install HAProxy 1.6 by adding the jessie-backports repository to your system.

```
~$ sudo echo deb http://httpredir.debian.org/debian jessie-backports main
    | sudo tee /etc/apt/sources.list.d/backports.list
```

Then update your apt package list.

```
~$ sudo apt update
```

Next, install the haproxy package, targeting the jessie-backports release.

```
~$ sudo apt install -y haproxy -t jessie-backports
```

At this point, you should be able to check that HAProxy was installed with the following command:

```
~$ /usr/sbin/haproxy -v
```

Verify that the service is running by passing the `status` parameter to the `service` command.

```
~$ sudo service haproxy status
```

You should see a status telling you that the service is now active and running.

```
haproxy.service - HAProxy Load Balancer Loaded:
loaded (/lib/systemd/system/haproxy.service; enabled)
Active: active (running) since Sat 2016-04-09 16:37:42 UTC; 1min 46s ago
```

You'll also find new files in the following locations:

Directory	What it's for
/usr/sbin	Contains the haproxy program.
/usr/share/lintian/overrides	Lintian is a Debian package checker. The file here overrides rules that would otherwise cause the HAProxy package to be flagged as having an error.
/usr/share/doc/haproxy	Documentation for HAproxy that can be viewed with `less` or `vi`.
/run/haproxy	Contains a UNIX socket that HAProxy binds to during startup.
/var/lib/haproxy	Contains data that HAProxy stores while running.
/etc/logrotate.d/haproxy	Configures HAProxy to use logrotate, which manages how logs are compressed and rotated.
/etc/default/haproxy	Contains a defaults file for HAProxy that can override aspects of how the service starts up, such as where to look for its configuration file.
/etc/haproxy	Contains the HAProxy configuration file and a directory where HTTP error pages are defined.
/etc/init.d	Contains the initialization script for the HAProxy service.

Throughout the book, we will be changing the configuration file located at /etc/haproxy/haproxy.cfg. This file can be edited in just about any text editor. Just be sure to restart the service afterwards by calling `sudo service haproxy restart`.

Installing on CentOS

To get HAProxy version 1.6 on CentOS 7, we'll first install version 1.5 with yum and then build the 1.6 source code ourselves and replace the HAProxy executable with the new one. Using yum to install the version 1.5 will get us 90% of the way there, taking care of creating the rest of the files, directories and initialization scripts. Begin by installing the haproxy package:

```
~$ sudo yum update
```

CHAPTER 2. INSTALLING HAPROXY

```
~$ sudo yum install haproxy -y
```

This package installs version 1.5, which you can verify with the command `haproxy -v`. We can get the source code for the latest version from the HAProxy website, http://www.haproxy.org. Download the 1.6 tarball to your home directory by using `wget`.

```
~$ cd ~
~$ wget http://www.haproxy.org/download/1.6/src/haproxy-1.6.9.tar.gz
```

Then extract the package using the `tar` command and navigate into the haproxy-1.6.9 directory:

```
~$ tar -zxvf haproxy-1.6.9.tar.gz
~$ cd haproxy-1.6.9
```

There are a few packages needed to successfully compile the project with the typical features: gcc for the compiler, pcre for Perl-compatible regular expressions, and openssl for SSL/TLS support. Install them with `yum` like so:

```
~$ sudo yum install gcc pcre-static pcre-devel openssl-devel -y
```

Set the flags to use when compiling the source code:

```
~$ make TARGET=linux2628 USE_OPENSSL=1 USE_PCRE=1 USE_ZLIB=1
```

Call `make install` to build the package.

```
~$ sudo make install
```

This copies the newly compiled haproxy executable into /usr/local/sbin. Copy it into /usr/sbin too:

```
~$ sudo cp /usr/local/sbin/haproxy /usr/sbin
```

CHAPTER 2. INSTALLING HAPROXY

You'll have to edit the HAProxy configuration file, /etc/haproxy/haproxy.cfg, before the service will start. To make things simple, delete the `frontend` and `backend` sections. We'll be adding them back in as we progress through the book.

After you've updated the haproxy.cfg file, the next step is to ensure that the service will be started after a reboot. We can use `systemctl enable` for this.

```
~$ sudo systemctl enable haproxy.service
```

Start the service with the following command:

```
~$ sudo service haproxy start
```

Verify that the service is running by passing the `status` parameter to the `service` command.

```
~$ sudo service haproxy status
```

You should see a status telling you that the service is now active and running.

```
haproxy.service - HAProxy Load Balancer
Loaded: loaded (/usr/lib/systemd/system/haproxy.service; enabled;
  vendor preset: disabled)
Active: active (running) since Sun 2016-07-24 18:33:07 UTC; 3s ago
```

We can also check that we're running HAProxy 1.6 with the following command:

```
~$ haproxy -v
```

You'll also find new files in the following locations:

Directory	What it's for
/etc/sysconfig	Contains a file where we can set options to pass to the HAProxy daemon.
/etc/logrotate.d/haproxy	Configures HAProxy to use logrotate, which manages how logs are compressed and rotated.

Directory	What it's for
/etc/haproxy	Contains the HAProxy configuration file and a directory where HTTP error pages are defined.
/var/lib/haproxy	Contains data that HAProxy stores while running.
/usr/sbin	Contains the haproxy program.
/usr/share/haproxy	Contains custom HTTP error pages.
/usr/local/sbin/haproxy	Contains a copy of the haproxy program.
/usr/local/doc/haproxy	Documentation for HAproxy that can be viewed with `less` or `vi`.

As we progress through the book, we'll be making changes to the HAProxy configuration file. Each time that we do, we'll need to restart the service by calling `sudo service haproxy restart`.

Installing with Docker

In this section, we'll use Docker to set up HAProxy and two instances of the NGINX Web server (pronounced engine X), each running in a separate Docker container. Docker is a fast way to spin up an environment where we can experiment with using HAProxy. I'll illustrate the setup on Ubuntu 16.04. To get started, update your system's packages.

```
~$ sudo apt update
```

To ensure that we can download packages over HTTPS, install the apt-transport-https and ca-certificates packages.

```
~$ sudo apt install apt-transport-https ca-certificates
```

Add the GPG key needed to access the Docker apt repository. These instructions can also be found in the online documentation for Docker at https://docs.docker.com/engine/installation.

```
~$ sudo apt-key adv --keyserver hkp://p80.pool.sks-keyservers.net:80
    --recv-keys 58118E89F3A912897C070ADBF76221572C52609D
```

Navigate to the /etc/apt/sources.list.d directory and verify that the docker.list file exists. If not, create it and make sure that it's writable. Then, add an entry to it that points to the Docker repository for your version of Ubuntu.

```
~$ cd /etc/apt/sources.list.d
~$ sudo touch docker.list
~$ sudo chmod o+w docker.list
~$ sudo echo deb https://apt.dockerproject.org/repo
    ubuntu-xenial main >> docker.list
```

I added ubuntu-xenial to the docker.list file, but you can also use ubuntu-wily, ubuntu-precise or ubuntu-trusty depending on the version of Ubuntu that you're installing Docker onto. Next, call `apt update` again.

```
~$ sudo apt update
```

Then install the Docker package.

```
~$ sudo apt install docker-engine -y
```

To check that it was installed successfully, check its version:

```
~$ docker -v
```

You must have version 1.7.0 or higher for the `docker network` commands that we'll use later.

Before we create the container that runs HAProxy, let's add an haproxy.cfg file. We will give the container access to see this file via a Docker volume. Volumes let a container access files and/or directories on the host machine. The file can go anywhere you like, but I'll place it under my home directory:

```
~$ cd ~
~$ touch haproxy.cfg
```

Update haproxy.cfg so that it contains the following:

```
defaults
  mode http
  timeout connect 5s
  timeout client 120s
  timeout server 120s

frontend mywebsite
  bind *:80
  default_backend webservers

backend webservers
  balance roundrobin
  server web1 web1:80 check
  server web2 web2:80 check
```

Now let's create the NGINX configuration and HTML files. As we will for the haproxy.cfg file, we'll use a Docker volume to share this with our container. I'll place it under a new directory called web1 relative to my home directory.

```
~$ cd ~
~$ mkdir web1
~$ cd web1
~$ touch nginx.conf
```

Edit nginx.conf so that it contains the following:

```
events {
  worker_connections 1024;
}

http {
  server {
    listen 80;

    # Prevent 304 responses
    if_modified_since off;
```

```
    location / {
      root /usr/share/nginx/html;
    }
  }
}
```

Also within the web1 directory, create another directory for the HTML files that NGINX will serve. Then add a file called index.html.

```
~$ mkdir html
~$ cd html
~$ touch index.html
```

Edit index.html to contain whatever you like, but it's helpful to include some message that lets you to know that you're looking at web1. Here's an example:

```
<!DOCTYPE html>
<html lang="en">
  <head>
    <meta charset="utf-8" />
    <title>Web 1</title>
  </head>
  <body>
    <h1>Web 1</h1>
  </body>
</hml>
```

We'll want two containers running NGINX so that we can load balance them. Repeat the steps that we took to create the web1 directory and files, but replace web1 with web2. We can use the `cp` and `sed` commands to make this quick and easy.

```
~$ cd ~
~$ cp -r web1 web2
~$ cd web2/html
~$ sed -i -e 's/Web 1/Web 2/g' index.html
```

CHAPTER 2. INSTALLING HAPROXY

Before we create our Docker containers, let's create an internal network that the Docker containers can use to communicate with one another. We'll name it my_network. Note that this will be a network that only Docker can see and won't affect other real or virtual networks.

```
~$ sudo docker network create -d bridge my_network
```

Now we're ready to create our containers. The following two commands will initialize Docker containers for our web1 and web2 NGINX websites:

```
~$ sudo docker run -d -v ~/web1/nginx.conf:/etc/nginx/nginx.conf
    -v ~/web1/html:/usr/share/nginx/html --net my_network --name web1 nginx

~$ sudo docker run -d -v ~/web2/nginx.conf:/etc/nginx/nginx.conf
    -v ~/web2/html:/usr/share/nginx/html --net my_network --name web2 nginx
```

Next, create the HAProxy container with the following command:

```
~$ sudo docker run -d -v ~/haproxy.cfg:/usr/local/etc/haproxy/haproxy.cfg
    -p 80:80 --net my_network --name lb1 haproxy
```

You can now call `sudo docker ps -a` to see that our containers are created and working. You should see something like this:

```
IMAGE    COMMAND                STATUS          PORTS              NAMES
nginx    "nginx -g 'daemon off" Up 2 minutes    80/tcp             web1
nginx    "nginx -g 'daemon off" Up 28 seconds   80/tcp             web2
haproxy  "haproxy -f /usr/loca" Up 3 seconds    0.0.0.0:80->80/tcp lb1
```

At this point, we have HAProxy load balancing two Web servers. If we visit localhost, we should see the webpage alternate between Web 1 and Web 2. If you're running this example on a Vagrant VM, and you've set up a private virtual network, then you should be able to browse port 80 at the VM's assigned IP address to see the website. We can edit the haproxy.cfg file at any time from our home directory and then reload it by calling **restart** on the Docker container.

```
~$ sudo docker restart lb1
```

We can also change the NGINX files and restart the web1 and web2 containers. To stop a container, call `docker stop [container name]`. To remove a container after you've stopped it, call `docker rm [container name]`.

Summary

In this chapter, we learned how to use Vagrant to make setting up a virtual machine easy. We installed HAProxy on several distributions of Linux including Debian, Ubuntu and CentOS. Each comes with a ready-made package that will install all the essential components, but if we want to run the latest version we may have to build the source code.

Docker gives us a convenient way to set up an entire test environment including load balancer and backend Web servers, all running on a single host operating system, but isolated within their own Docker containers. Using Docker volumes lets us edit the HAProxy configuration file from our host machine and then restart the container to have it take effect.

Chapter 3

Basics

For most of the book, we'll be discussing features of HAProxy that require us to edit the /etc/haproxy/haproxy.cfg configuration file. This one file controls almost all of HAProxy's behavior and is where we'd turn settings on and off. It's important to understand its structure, since, after this chapter, we'll be focusing on individual configuration directives rather than the file as a whole. The sections here will lay down the groundwork for the rest of the book, giving you the context for where settings could be plugged in.

In this chapter, we'll cover the following topics:

- Setting up a simple reverse proxy
- Load balancing several servers
- Setting the load-balancing mode
- Capturing the client's source IP for logging
- Matching requests and responses against criteria and then taking action based on them
- Enabling the HAProxy stats page

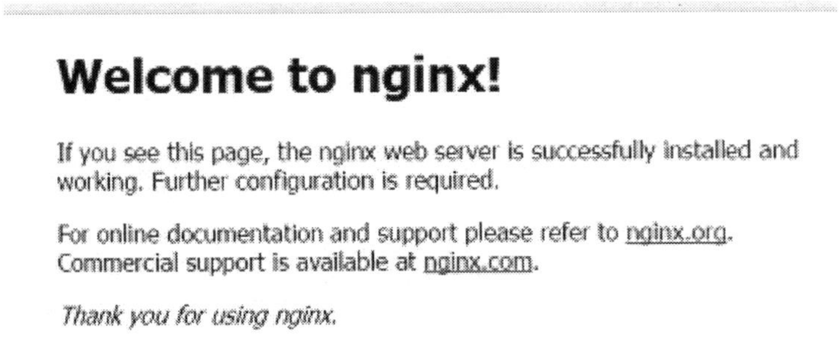

> **Welcome to nginx!**
>
> If you see this page, the nginx web server is successfully installed and working. Further configuration is required.
>
> For online documentation and support please refer to nginx.org.
> Commercial support is available at nginx.com.
>
> *Thank you for using nginx.*

Figure 3.1: Proxied webpage

Proxying basics

Let's start out with discussing how we would use HAProxy to proxy requests to a single Web server. On Ubuntu, an easy Web server to install is called NGINX. Use the following **apt** commands to update your system's list of packages and then to install it:

```
~$ sudo apt update
~$ sudo apt install nginx -y
```

The NGINX configuration file can be found at /etc/nginx/nginx.conf and some default HTML files are added to /usr/share/nginx/html. Without any modification, a default Welcome to nginx! webpage will be served at http://localhost, which listens on port 80.

Now let's put HAProxy in front of this Web server. Since we're just trying things out, it's fine to install HAProxy on the same machine where we installed NGINX, although in a real-world scenario, they'd likely be on separate machines. Refer to the earlier instructions for how to install HAProxy. Once installed, view the file /etc/haproxy/haproxy.cfg. You will see the following default configuration:

```
global
  log /dev/log local0
  log /dev/log local1 notice
  chroot /var/lib/haproxy
  stats socket /run/haproxy/admin.sock mode 660 level admin
```

CHAPTER 3. BASICS

```
    stats timeout 30s
    user haproxy
    group haproxy
    daemon

    # Default SSL material locations
    ca-base /etc/ssl/certs
    crt-base /etc/ssl/private

    # Default ciphers to use on SSL-enabled listening sockets.
    # For more information, see ciphers(1SSL). This list is from:
    #   https://hynek.me/articles/hardening-your-web-servers-ssl-ciphers/
    ssl-default-bind-ciphers ECDH+AESGCM:DH+AESGCM:ECDH+AES256:DH+AES256:
       ECDH+AES128:DH+AES:ECDH+3DES:DH+3DES:RSA+AESGCM:RSA+AES:RSA+3DES:!aNULL:
       !MD5:!DSS
    ssl-default-bind-options no-sslv3

defaults
    log global
    mode http
    option httplog
    option dontlognull
    timeout connect 5000
    timeout client  50000
    timeout server  50000
    errorfile 400 /etc/haproxy/errors/400.http
    errorfile 403 /etc/haproxy/errors/403.http
    errorfile 408 /etc/haproxy/errors/408.http
    errorfile 500 /etc/haproxy/errors/500.http
    errorfile 502 /etc/haproxy/errors/502.http
    errorfile 503 /etc/haproxy/errors/503.http
    errorfile 504 /etc/haproxy/errors/504.http
```

The `global` section contains settings that apply to the HAProxy process itself. It breaks down as follows:

- The `log` directives set up syslog logging of incoming requests and any errors that occur.

- `chroot` runs the HAProxy process in a Linux chroot jail for enhanced security.

- The `stats` directives set up a Unix domain socket that we can use to interact with HAProxy from the command line, such as to enable and disable the proxies we set up.

- The `user` and `group` directives define which system user and group the HAProxy process will run as. You can verify this with the command `ps -eo user,group,args | grep haproxy`.

- `daemon` tells HAProxy to run in the background.

The rest of the settings in the `global` section:

- `ca-base`
- `crt-base`
- `ssl-default-bind-ciphers`
- `ssl-default-bind-options`

relate to using SSL termination, which is a topic we'll cover in depth later. A few of the lines have a hash sign (#) in front of them. These are comments that will be ignored by HAProxy. You can use comments to writes notes about what you have done in the configuration. Any line that begins with a hash will not be evaluated.

In the `defaults` section, we can configure settings that are reused across all of the proxies that we'll define. Here's how these settings break down:

- `log global` tells each proxy to use the logging configuration that was set up in the `global` section.

- `mode http` tells each proxy to operate at Layer 7 (`http`) rather than Layer 4 (`tcp`), which gives it the ability to inspect HTTP messages.

- `option httplog` turns on verbose logging of HTTP messages.

- `option dontlognull` skips logging when a request doesn't send any data.

- `timeout connect` sets the maximum number of milliseconds to wait for a successful connection to a backend server.

- `timeout client` sets the maximum number of milliseconds to wait for a client, such as a Web browser, to respond when it is expected to.

- `timeout server` sets the maximum number of milliseconds to wait for a backend server to respond when it is expected to.

- Each `errorfile` directive points to an HTML file on disk that will be served when HAProxy encounters an error during its own processing. You can replace these files with your own. These are not returned when your Web servers respond with an HTTP error status of their own, such as 404 Not Found or 500 Server Error. You would see the HAProxy 503 Service Unavailable page, for example, when no backend servers are up.

It's fine to keep these settings. Below them, we'll add a few new sections. Besides `global` and `defaults`, there are three other types of sections you can add, and you may add as many of each as you want.

- A `frontend` defines a reverse proxy that will listen for incoming requests on a certain IP and port.

- A `backend` defines a pool of servers that the `frontend` will forward requests to.

- A `listen` section is a shorthand notation that combines the features of a `frontend` and a `backend` into one.

Let's define a `frontend` first. We'll have it listen on the IP address 127.0.0.1 at port 81, since NGINX is already running on port 80 on this machine. Add the following snippet to the bottom of the haproxy.cfg file:

```
frontend myproxy
    bind 127.0.0.1:81
    default_backend mywebservers
```

The `bind` directive creates a new proxy that listens on the given IP address and port. We can give a specific IP or an asterisk, *, which means any IP address configured on this machine.

```
frontend myproxy
   bind *:81
   default_backend mywebservers
```

We can also omit the IP address altogether, which means the same as if we'd given an asterisk.

```
bind :81
```

We can have as many `bind` directives in our `frontend` as we want. For example, the following proxy would listen for incoming requests on IP addresses 127.0.0.1 and 10.0.0.5 at port 81:

```
frontend myproxy
   bind 127.0.0.1:81
   bind 10.0.0.5:81
   default_backend mywebservers
```

After you've made changes to haproxy.cfg, you can validate its correctness by calling the haproxy executable, passing the path to the configuration file with the `-f` flag and checking for errors with the `-c` flag.

```
~$ haproxy -f /etc/haproxy/haproxy.cfg -c
```

At this point, we will get an error because we haven't defined a group of servers to proxy the requests to. You should see the following message telling you that our configuration isn't complete yet:

> [ALERT] 154/162841 (19533) : Proxy 'myproxy': unable to find required default_backend: 'mywebservers'.

Our `frontend` is configured, via its `default_backend` directive, to forward requests to a pool of servers defined in a `backend` section called mywebservers. Let's go ahead and define that. Add the following snippet below the `frontend` section:

```
backend mywebservers
   server nginx1 127.0.0.1:80
```

CHAPTER 3. BASICS

Each `server` directive sets a label, IP and port for the target server. In this example, I decided to assign our Web server a label of nginx1. This is only visible to the current `backend`, so as long as you don't duplicate it within this section, you're good-to-go. Since NGINX is running on the same machine as HAProxy, I set the server's IP to the loopback address, 127.0.0.1, and its port to 80. Altogether, our haproxy.cfg file now looks like this:

```
global
  log /dev/log local0
  log /dev/log local1 notice
  chroot /var/lib/haproxy
  stats socket /run/haproxy/admin.sock mode 660 level admin
  stats timeout 30s
  user haproxy
  group haproxy
  daemon

  # Default SSL material locations
  ca-base /etc/ssl/certs
  crt-base /etc/ssl/private

  # Default ciphers to use on SSL-enabled listening sockets.
  # For more information, see ciphers(1SSL). This list is from:
  #   https://hynek.me/articles/hardening-your-web-servers-ssl-ciphers/
  ssl-default-bind-ciphers ECDH+AESGCM:DH+AESGCM:ECDH+AES256:DH+AES256:
    ECDH+AES128:DH+AES:ECDH+3DES:DH+3DES:RSA+AESGCM:RSA+AES:RSA+3DES:!aNULL
    :!MD5:!DSS
  ssl-default-bind-options no-sslv3

defaults
  log global
  mode http
  option httplog
  option dontlognull
  timeout connect 5000
  timeout client  50000
  timeout server  50000
  errorfile 400 /etc/haproxy/errors/400.http
```

```
    errorfile 403 /etc/haproxy/errors/403.http
    errorfile 408 /etc/haproxy/errors/408.http
    errorfile 500 /etc/haproxy/errors/500.http
    errorfile 502 /etc/haproxy/errors/502.http
    errorfile 503 /etc/haproxy/errors/503.http
    errorfile 504 /etc/haproxy/errors/504.http

frontend myproxy
    bind *:81
    default_backend mywebservers

backend mywebservers
    server nginx1 127.0.0.1:80
```

Try verifying the configuration file again with `haproxy -f /etc/haproxy/haproxy.cfg -c`. This time you should see:

> Configuration file is valid

Great! Now let's restart the HAProxy service so that our changes take effect. We have to do this any time we edit the haproxy.cfg file.

```
~$ sudo service haproxy restart
```

In your browser, or using `curl`, navigate to http://localhost:81, and you should see the same NGINX webpage that we saw before. This time, however, the request is being proxied through HAProxy before being sent to the Web server!

For the sake of completeness, let's change our file so that it uses a single `listen` directive instead of a `frontend` and `backend`. A `listen` combines the features of both. It would look like this:

```
listen myproxy
    bind *:81
    server nginx1 127.0.0.1:80
```

Restart the HAProxy service with `sudo service haproxy restart` and then check that we get the same result as before when we visit http://localhost:81.

Load balancing basics

We've seen how to forward a request through a `frontend` proxy to a `backend` that has only one server. To get the most out of HAProxy though, we'll want to distribute the load across many servers. This is actually very simple: We just add more `server` directives. Here's an example where our mywebservers `backend` shares the traffic equally among three Web servers by using the roundrobin algorithm:

```
frontend myproxy
  bind *:80
  default_backend mywebservers

backend mywebservers
  balance roundrobin
  server webserver1 192.168.50.30:80
  server webserver2 192.168.50.31:80
  server webserver3 192.168.50.32:80
```

We can picture a request as flowing from the user to the load balancer, and then to one of the Web servers. When the request arrives at the load balancer, it is first accepted by a `frontend`, which then passes it to a `backend` pool of servers. In the `backend`, HAProxy must choose one of the Web servers to handle the request. The `balance` directive specifies which algorithm to use for deciding which server should be used. There are a few algorithms to choose from, including roundrobin, which is the default if we don't set one.

When we use the roundrobin load-balancing algorithm, requests go to each server in a rotation in the order that the `server` directives are listed. So, webserver1 gets the first request, webserver2 gets the second, webserver3 gets the third and then the next request goes back to webserver1. We can add as many `server` directives as we want to a single `backend`. They will take turns responding to requests. We'll discuss this and other algorithms in more detail later.

We can set up different `backend` sections containing pools of servers to handle requests for each of our websites. In the following example, when we receive a request on IP address 10.0.0.5, we forward it to servers in the myshoes_servers `backend`. When we receive a request on IP address 10.0.0.6, we send it to the myhats_servers `backend`. Each contains its own group of servers.

```
frontend myshoes_website
  bind 10.0.0.5:80
  default_backend myshoes_servers

frontend myhats_website
  bind 10.0.0.6:80
  default_backend myhats_servers

backend myshoes_servers
  balance roundrobin
  server server1 192.168.50.30:80
  server server2 192.168.50.31:80

backend myhats_servers
  balance roundrobin
  server server1 192.168.50.40:80
  server server2 192.168.50.41:80
```

Notice that we're binding our proxies to IP addresses in the 10.0.0.0/24 range, but keeping our backend servers on a different network: 192.168.50.0/24. This is just to show you that you can expose one set of IP addresses, probably public IPs, to your clients, while using different, probably internal-only, IP addresses for your Web servers, databases, and the like. That way, nobody from outside the corporate network can connect directly to our Web servers. Also, from the outside, it's impossible to tell that our website is backed by multiple load-balanced servers. There's also no way that an outsider would know that we're using HAProxy. To them, it will seem as if they're accessing a single, very powerful, server.

The machine where HAProxy is running will need to accept requests at the IP addresses that we bound to in the `frontend` sections. We can add them to a network interface with the Linux `ip address add` command. For example, in the following snippet, we use the `ip address add` command to bind 10.0.0.5 to the eth1 network interface:

```
~$ ip address add 10.0.0.5 dev eth1
```

We would do this for each IP address where a `frontend`, also known as a proxy, is listening.

TCP vs HTTP mode

Load balancers typically come in two flavors: those that operate at the transport layer, which is layer 4 of the Open Systems Interconnection (OSI) model and those that operate higher-up the network stack at the application layer, also known as layer 7. The layers of the OSI model look like this:

Layer	What happens
1 - Physical	Streams of bits are transmitted as electronic signals over wires and other physical devices.
2 - Data Link	Converts the electronic signals from the physical layer into packets that the network layer can understand and vice versa. Protocols used by routers, NICs and other network devices are defined here.
3 - Network	Defines how a network device will know where to route data to and also whether incoming data is addressed to the current device.
4 - Transport	Ensures that multiple applications on a computer can communicate over a network at the same time. To do so, data for each application is associated with a unique port on the computer.
5 - Session	Allows applications that are connected over a network to participate in a shared, ongoing conversation, much like a phone conversation between two people.
6 - Presentation	Responsible for transforming data between machines that may represent it differently, such as converting line endings between Linux and Windows.
7 - Application	Specifies how data is interpreted by various kinds of network applications. For example, HTTP is a protocol used by Web browsers for sending and receiving webpages.

While some load balancers can only operate at Layer 4, routing data to servers based solely on the source and destination IP address and port, HAProxy can also operate higher up the stack at Layer 7. This gives it the ability to open HTTP requests and see headers, cookies, and message bodies. It can then make smarter decisions about which server to forward the request to based on what it finds.

You can choose to use HAProxy as a Layer 4 load balancer if you like, which uses less processing power and, in some cases, may be all you need. For example, when load balancing several replicas of a MySQL database, which does not use HTTP, we can simply operate at TCP, layer 4. To do so, set `mode tcp` in your `frontend` and `backend`, like so:

```
frontend mysql
  mode tcp
  bind *:3306
  default_backend dbservers

backend dbservers
  mode tcp
  server db1 192.168.50.10:3306
  server db2 192.168.50.11:3307
```

The `mode` defaults to `tcp` if not set. Even for services that communicate over HTTP, we can still use `mode tcp`. You might do this if you only wanted to use HAProxy's TCP-based load balancing features without all of the smarts of inspecting the HTTP traffic. However, if you would like to take advantage of the advanced layer 7 capabilities, use `mode http` instead.

```
frontend mywebsite
  mode http
  bind *:80
  default_backend mywebservers

backend mywebservers
  mode http
  server webserver1 192.168.40.10:80
  server webserver2 192.168.40.11:80
```

Some things that we can do when operating in this mode that we can't do in `tcp` mode include:

- routing traffic to particular servers based on the URL, HTTP headers or body
- modifying the URL and headers

CHAPTER 3. BASICS

- reading and setting cookies
- determining the health of a server based on its HTTP responses

You can also set a `mode` in the `defaults` section so that it applies to all. If you do, it can be overridden by each `frontend`, `backend` and `listen` section. We can use a mix of layer 4 and layer 7 load balancing within our configuration file. Just make sure that the modes match between any frontend proxy and the corresponding backend pool of servers.

Capturing the client's IP address

One bad thing about using a reverse proxy is that to our upstream servers, it looks like the request originated at the proxy instead of from the client. Oftentimes, we want to capture the client's source IP address in our Web server's logs. We don't want to log our proxy's IP address. To solve this problem, we can add a header called X-Forwarded-For to the incoming request before it's passed along to the Web server. Then the server can look for and parse this header to get the original, client IP address.

To enable this header, add `option forwardfor` to the `frontend`.

```
frontend myproxy
  mode http
  bind *:80
  option forwardfor
  default_backend mywebservers
```

We can also add an `option forwardfor` directive to the `defaults` section so that it applies across the board to all proxies. When we use this directive, HAProxy adds an X-Forwarded-For header to all incoming requests and sets its value to the client's IP address. If there's a chance that the header might already be set by another proxy before it gets to HAProxy, then we can append `if-none` to say that we only want to add it if it's not there.

```
option forwardfor if-none
```

The X-Forwarded-For header is not officially-approved in the HTTP specification. It's just so widely used that it's an unofficial standard. However, a new header called Forwarded was officially proposed in RFC 7239 and serves the same purpose. If you want to send a Forwarded header to capture the client's IP address, you can do so by using the `http-request set-header` directive instead of, or in addition to, `option forwardfor`. In the following snippet, we add the Forwarded header to all incoming requests. Note that it uses a specialized, key-value format: `for=%[src]`.

```
frontend myproxy
  mode http
  bind *:80
  default_backend mywebservers
  option forwardfor
  http-request set-header Forwarded for=%[src]
```

Whether we're using the X-Forwarded-For or the Forwarded header, we can only add headers when we're using `mode http`. So what can we do if we're operating in `mode tcp`? In that case we can use the PROXY Protocol. The PROXY Protocol sends the client's source IP, the proxy's IP, and the source and destination ports when the TCP connection is first established. To enable this feature, add a `send-proxy` parameter to a `server` directive. In the following example, we send the PROXY Protocol data to the webserver1 Web server.

```
frontend myproxy
  mode tcp
  bind *:80
  default_backend mywebservers

backend mywebservers
  mode tcp
  server webserver1 192.168.40.10:80 send-proxy
```

The information it sends looks like this:

```
PROXY TCP4 192.168.50.22 192.168.40.10 10970 80
```

In this case, my client IP address happens to be 192.168.50.22 and the IP address where HAProxy is running is 192.168.40.10. The webserver1 server has to be ready

CHAPTER 3. BASICS

to accept this information. If not, you'll get errors. For example, NGINX can accept the data by adding a `proxy_protocol` parameter to its `listen` directive. Then we can log it by changing the `log_format` directive to log the `$proxy_protocol_addr` parameter and adding an `accept_log` directive that references this new format. Here is an updated /etc/nginx/nginx.conf file:

```
http {
  log_format proxyformat
    '$proxy_protocol_addr - $remote_user [$time_local] '
    '"$request" $status $body_bytes_sent '
    '"$http_referer" "$http_user_agent"';

  access_log /var/log/nginx/proxylog.log proxyformat;

  server {
    listen 80 proxy_protocol;
    location / {
      root /usr/share/nginx/html;
    }
  }
}
```

Then we can see that the client's true IP address, 192.168.50.22, is logged rather than the load balancer's when we view NGINX's logs at /var/log/nginx/proxylog.log:

```
192.168.50.22 - - [16/Jun/2016:17:54:32 +0000] "GET / HTTP/1.1" 200 160 "-"
  "Mozilla/5.0 (Windows NT 10.0; WOW64) AppleWebKit/537.36 (KHTML, like Gecko)
  Chrome/51.0.2704.84 Safari/537.36"
```

Beware that some Web servers, such as IIS, don't support the Proxy Protocol.

Using ACLs

In HAProxy, an Access Control List (ACL) is a set of criteria that we try to match incoming requests or responses against. If the criteria match, we take an action such as directing the client to a specific server, denying their request, or changing the

URL that they're asking for. The type of information we try to match on includes the client's source IP address, the protocol used, whether a specific cookie or HTTP header exists, and the URL that was requested. This ability to inspect the data and match against rules opens the door to a lot of the higher-level intelligence of HAProxy.

In the /etc/haproxy/haproxy.cfg HAProxy configuration file, we define a set of criteria by adding an `acl` directive with a name and the rules to match on. This always involves using a fetch method, which is a built-in helper for getting information about the request or response. You can get a full list of fetch methods at http://cbonte.github.io/haproxy-dconv/configuration-1.6.html#7.3.2. For example, the `src` fetch method gets the client's source IP address. In the following example, we've added an `acl` called is_localhost that checks if the source IP is 127.0.0.1:

```
frontend mywebsite
  bind *:80
  acl is_localhost src 127.0.0.1
  default_backend webservers
```

If `src` equals 127.0.0.1, then the is_localhost `acl` will get a value of true. We can use that when deciding which `backend` to send the client to. The `use_backend` chooses an alternate `backend` if the given `acl` is true. Otherwise, we send the client to the default webservers `backend`.

```
frontend mywebsite
  bind *:80
  acl is_localhost src 127.0.0.1
  use_backend localhost_server if is_localhost
  default_backend webservers
```

In addition to using `if`, we can also use `unless`:

```
use_backend webservers unless is_localhost
default_backend localhost_server
```

We can also put the `acl` onto the same line as the `use_backend`. In that case, the criteria are surrounded with curly braces. Having it on a separate line means we can reuse it in other places, but having it all on one line is convenient if we only use it once.

```
frontend mywebsite
  bind *:80
  use_backend localhost_server if { src 127.0.0.1 }
  default_backend webservers
```

We can also match against multiple ACLs at the same time. An and is implied when we list them one after another. In fact, putting the word and between two ACLs would be considered an invalid configuration. In the next example, we have an **acl** called is_localhost that checks whether the **src** fetch method returns a value that's equal to 127.0.0.1. We have another **acl** called is_get that checks whether the **method** fetch method returns a value that's equal to GET. Then, on the **use_backend** line, we send the request to the localhost_server **backend** if both is_localhost and is_get are true.

```
acl is_localhost src 127.0.0.1
acl is_get method GET
use_backend localhost_server if is_localhost is_get
```

If we wanted to send the request to the localhost_server backend if the IP address is 127.0.0.1 or if the method is GET, we'd specify an **or** operator between the two ACLs.

```
acl is_localhost src 127.0.0.1
acl is_get method GET
use_backend localhost_server if is_localhost or is_get
```

Of course, that would send all GET requests to the localhost_server, but you get the idea!

Enabling the HAProxy stats page

HAProxy comes with a built-in webpage that displays information about your proxies and backend servers. The stats page will capture the number of active sessions for each server, the number of requests that have been queued, whether there have been any errors and whether a server is reporting as up or down. Note that this

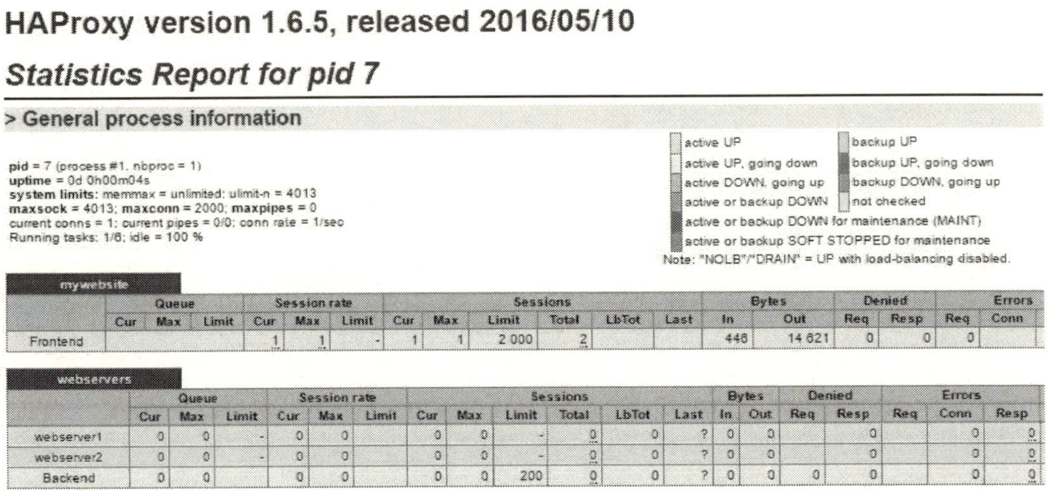

Figure 3.2: The stats webpage

page is only available if you have at least one pair of `frontend` and `backend` sections listening in `http` mode.

Edit your /etc/haproxy/haproxy.cfg file so that it has a `stats enable` directive in its `defaults` section. This will enable the stats webpage.

```
defaults
  stats enable
```

Remember to restart the HAProxy service after changing the configuration file by calling `sudo service haproxy restart`. We can see the stats page by navigating to the URL /haproxy?stats from any IP address where a `frontend` is bound. It looks like this:

We can change the URL by setting the `stats uri` directive to another path like /report or /stats?overview or really anything that makes sense for you. The page refreshes itself every five seconds, but this can be changed with the `stats refresh` directive. It accepts a time duration, such as 10s for ten seconds or 1m for one minute. In the following example, I change the URL to /report and the refresh rate to 30 seconds:

CHAPTER 3. BASICS

```
defaults
  stats enable
  stats uri /report
  stats refresh 30s
```

We can restrict access to this page by adding a `stats auth` directive, specifying a username and password. This tells HAProxy to use Basic authentication and to prompt the user to log in when they visit the page.

```
stats auth admin:password1
```

In this case, the user would enter admin for the username and password1 for the password. You can grant access to more users by adding more `stats auth` directives. Basic authentication communicates in the clear using plain text, so it's best to enable SSL for this page. In order to control the protocol used, we'll dedicate a single proxy for serving the stats page. The easiest way to do that is to use a `listen` section and move our `stats` directives there, rather than having them in the `defaults` section. Here's an example where we've moved the stats configuration to a `listen` section that binds to port 9000 and uses SSL:

```
listen statspage
  bind *:9000 ssl crt /etc/ssl/certs/mycert.pem
  stats enable
  stats uri /report
  stats refresh 30s
  stats auth admin:password1
```

Now the webpage can be accessed on any IP address at port 9000, but only over HTTPS. We'll talk about setting up SSL termination later on. For now, just notice that we have to add the `ssl` parameter to our `bind` directive and reference our website's SSL certificate with the `crt` parameter. Creating a self-signed SSL certificate is outside the scope of this topic, but we'll cover it in chapter 9 in the section on SSL termination.

Let's talk about fine-tuning how the stats page is displayed. Each `listen`, `frontend` and `backend` is listed on the stats page. We can add some custom text for each one by adding a `description` directive to the corresponding section. In the following example, we add the `description` Our snazzy Web servers to the webservers `backend`.

webservers				Our snazzy Web servers								
	Queue			Session rate			Sessions					
	Cur	Max	Limit	Cur	Max	Limit	Cur	Max	Limit	Total	LbTot	Last
web1	0	0	-	0	0		0	0	-	0	0	?
web2	0	0	-	0	0		0	0	-	0	0	?
Backend	0	0		0	0		0	0	200	0	0	?

Figure 3.3: A stats page description

```
backend webservers
  description Our snazzy Web servers
  balance roundrobin
  server web1 172.18.0.2:80
  server web2 172.18.0.3:80
```

It will be displayed on the webpage above that group of servers:

We can also add text to the top of the page by adding a `description` directive to the `global` section and then adding the `stats show-desc` directive. The following will show Our awesome HAProxy Stats page:

```
global
  description Our awesome HAProxy Stats page

listen statspage
  bind *:9000 ssl crt /etc/ssl/certs/mycert.pem
  stats enable
  stats uri /report
  stats refresh 30s
  stats auth admin:password1
  stats show-desc
```

If we add the `stats show-legends` directive then hovering our mouse over a server on the webpage will display some additional information about it:

The stats page is great for seeing the status of our backend servers, but we can also control them through this page. When we add a `stats admin` directive, the page displays a checkbox next to each server and a dropdown menu that lets you perform an action on it. You must give an `if` or `unless` statement to restrict when to show

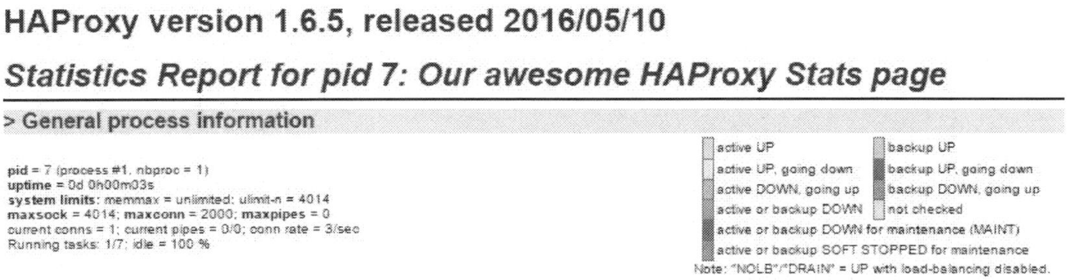

CHAPTER 3. BASICS

Figure 3.4: Displaying a global description

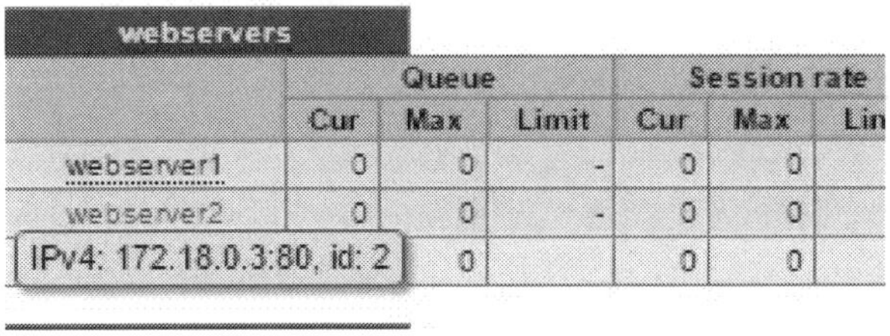

Figure 3.5: Displaying additional server information

these admin functions. You can just tell HAProxy to turn it on all the time by setting `if TRUE`.

```
listen statspage
  # other stats settings...
  stats admin if TRUE
```

Or we can restrict it so that it's only accessible when browsed via localhost by setting `if LOCALHOST`. Here's what it will look like:

It helps to set the `stats refresh` directive so that the page refreshes are far enough apart to give you enough time to select a server and apply the action. If you're curious about what each function does, here is a guide:

Action	What it does
Set state to READY	Enables the server, cancelling DRAIN and MAINT modes

Action	What it does
Set state to DRAIN	Disables any traffic to the server except those from persistent connections and continues to send health checks
Set state to MAINT	Disables all traffic to the server and turns off health checks
Health: disable checks	Disables sending health checks to the server
Health: enable checks	Enables sending health checks to the server
Health: force UP	Sets the server's health check status to up
Health: force NOLB	Sets the server's health check status as nolb, which means it will not accept new non-persistent connections
Health: force DOWN	Sets the server's health check status to down
Agent: disable checks	When an auxiliary health check is configured via the `agent-check` directive, this disables those checks
Agent: enable checks	When an auxiliary health check is configured via the `agent-check` directive, this enables those checks
Agent: force UP	Sets auxiliary agent checks to a status of up
Agent: force DOWN	Sets auxiliary agent checks to a status of down
Kill Sessions	Terminates all the sessions attached to the server

The stats page can be consumed in comma-separated-values (CSV) format, which is helpful to monitoring tools like Nagios. By appending ;csv to the end of the URL, we get a CSV version of the page. There's also a link on the stats page to this called CSV export. So, we could set up a monitoring script that reads this page for real-time notifications of downtime. A Google search will likely turn up scripts to do this that others have already written.

Summary

In this chapter, we learned the basics of using HAProxy. By binding to an IP address in a `frontend` and sending requests to a single server in a `backend`, we get the benefits of a reverse proxy. This layer of abstraction conceals the true structure of our internal network from outsiders and allows us to modify our backend server without the client knowing. A `bind` statement can listen on a specific IP and port or

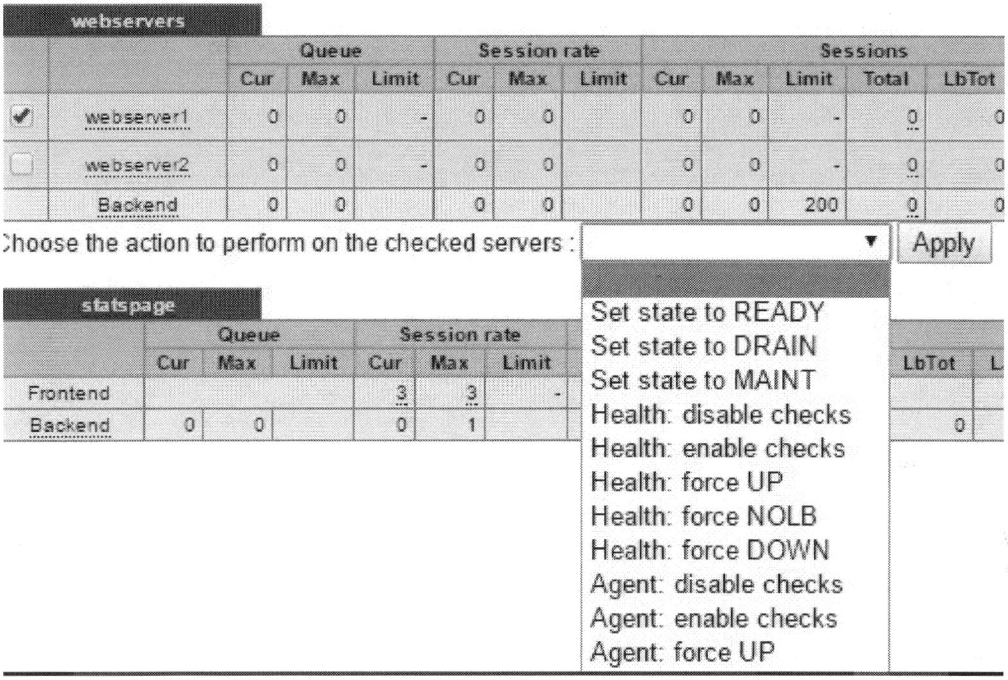

Figure 3.6: Enabling admin mode

on all IP addresses assigned to the machine. A `frontend` can also bind to multiple IP addresses and ports.

We saw that to enable HAProxy's load balancing capabilities, we would simply add more `server` directives to a `backend` and choose a load-balancing algorithm. Load balancing many servers is a great way to distribute the load of incoming traffic. Load balancing comes in two modes: `tcp` for layer 4 basic IP routing and `http` for layer 7 routing based on HTTP messages.

Because we don't want our upstream Web servers logging our proxy's IP address, we will want a way to capture the client's source IP. To do so, we can use the `option forwardfor` directive or set the Forwarded header. When we're using `mode tcp`, we can use the PROXY Protocol to pass this information.

We learned that ACLs give us a way to match requests and responses against criteria so that we can then take certain actions. A lot of HAProxy's power comes from using this built-in intelligence. We can also get a lot of good information about the health of our proxies and backend servers by setting up the HAProxy stats page. We can control the URL, refresh rate and authentication of this page and customize descriptions for the various sections. One big motivation for using the stats page is for its ability to send commands to HAProxy, such as to enable and disable servers.

Chapter 4

Load Balancing Algorithms

When HAProxy receives a request, it must decide which server to send it to. Different behavior is enabled by specifying one of the available load-balancing algorithms. Each has pros and cons and works better for some situations than others. In fact, within the same configuration file, we can have some services use one algorithm and others use another.

In this chapter, we'll cover the following topics:

- The roundrobin algorithm
- The weighted roundrobin algorithm
- The leastconn algorithm
- The weighted leastconn algorithm
- The hash uri algorithm
- The first available algorithm

Roundrobin algorithm

The roundrobin load-balancing algorithm is the default if you don't set the `balance` directive. It is, by far, the simplest to understand and makes for a good choice if you don't want any surprises regarding how the traffic will be split among servers.

It is also the most balanced, meaning that your servers will each receive an equal amount of traffic. If you have two servers, each will get half of the traffic. If you have four, they'll each get a quarter of the traffic.

How it works is that incoming requests are forwarded to each server sequentially, in a rotation. In the following example, I've set up a `backend` section that explicitly declares, with the `balance roundrobin` directive, that it will use the roundrobin algorithm.

```
frontend mywebsite
  bind 10.0.0.5:80
  default_backend webservers

backend webservers
  balance roundrobin
  server web1 192.168.50.10:80
  server web2 192.168.50.11:80
```

Here, web1 would get the first request. The second would go to web2. The third would go back to web1, etc. This works well when serving content that takes a short and consistent amount of time to generate, such as static web pages. It might not work as well for requests that take a variable amount of time to process, such as database queries because one server might become bogged down with more long-running requests than the other. The roundrobin algorithm doesn't check how much load is on a server before sending the next request. If it is that server's turn, it's getting it.

A `balance` directive can be set in a `backend` section or globally in the `defaults` section. If it's set in the `defaults`, it can be overridden within a `backend` to use a different algorithm.

Be sure to have enough servers to accommodate traffic if one or two are taken offline for maintenance or because of a failure. For example, you'd want to ensure that if web1 fails, that all of the traffic isn't sent to web2 if that's more than it can handle. In that case, you may want to have at least three servers defined in the `backend`.

Weighted roundrobin algorithm

Roundrobin load balancing means that each server gets an equal amount of traffic because requests are sent to each one in a simple rotation. We can, however, distribute the traffic more heavily to some by assigning a `weight` to them. This is handy when some of your servers are running on faster hardware, for example. In that case, to take advantage of the extra power, you might want to send twice as many requests to those servers.

Each `server` in a backend can specify a `weight`, between 0 and 256, that determines the proportion of traffic it should receive. The number of requests that are forwarded to a server will be calculated by dividing its weight by the sum of all weights. So, in the following example, web1 will get 1/4 of the traffic and web2 will get 3/4. By default, servers have a weight of 1.

```
backend webservers
  balance roundrobin
  server web1 192.168.50.10:80 weight 1
  server web2 192.168.50.11:80 weight 3
```

A weight of 0 would prevent any traffic from going to that server. This can be useful when doing maintenance. However, the same can be accomplished by adding the `disabled` parameter to a `server` line, which is arguably better in terms of readability. Here's an example that uses the `disabled` parameter:

```
server web1 192.168.50.10:80 weight 1 disabled
```

Another creative way to use weights is to deploy a new website feature to only one of your servers and then send a small amount of traffic, maybe 1/10, to it. That way, if the new feature doesn't do well, only 1/10 of the requests were affected. This technique, known as canary deployments works best when clients are sent to one, and only one, server for the duration of their session. This can be accomplished with server persistence, which we'll cover later in the book. You can also dynamically change the weight of a server from the command line, which we'll also cover later, to slowly ratchet up the number of clients that see the feature.

Leastconn algorithm

The roundrobin algorithm shares traffic equally amongst servers, but doesn't take into account how busy a server is. Even weighted roundrobin, which changes the proportion of traffic to a server, can't adapt when a server becomes overwhelmed with connections due to circumstances like long-running database queries. So, even if a server is already servicing many requests, new ones will continue to pour into it. To solve this problem, the leastconn algorithm continuously checks how many active TCP connections each server has and sends the next request to the server with the fewest.

In the next example, I've set the `balance leastconn` directive in the `database_replicas` `backend`. Requests will go to the database server with the fewest connections. Load-balancing several read-only replicas of a database is a good use-case for this, allowing us to horizontally scale our reads so that we avoid bogging down any particular server if it is processing many long-running queries.

```
frontend my_readonly_database
  mode tcp
  bind *:1433
  default_backend database_replicas

backend database_replicas
  mode tcp
  balance leastconn
  server db1 192.168.50.15:1433
  server db2 192.168.50.16:1433
```

Here, we're load-balancing two Microsoft SQL Server databases. Since they listen on TCP port 1433 and don't communicate over HTTP, we're using `mode tcp` and binding to port 1433 in both the `frontend` and `backend`. SQL Server has a feature called transactional replication in which changes to a master database are immediately copied to secondary, read-only databases. If your application reads from your database more than it writes to it, which is typical of Web applications, then splitting reads from writes and load balancing several read-only replicas makes sense.

Something else to consider when using leastconn is how to prevent the server from being overloaded when it first comes online. Let's suppose that your server fails or is taken offline for maintenance. When it's put back into action, using the leastconn load-balancing algorithm, since it now has the fewest connections, all of the new requests will be sent to it. If there's a lot of traffic that means it will get a rush of clients trying to connect. That may be enough to overwhelm the server's connection limit or to max out its resources. This can be especially problematic when you're experiencing a spike in traffic that's overwhelming all of your servers.

To avoid this, add the `slowstart` parameter to the `server` directive. It specifies an amount of time during which it will ramp up connections when first starting up, giving it time to finish some requests along the way. In the following example, we give each server a 60-second ramp-up time after coming online.

```
backend databases
  mode tcp
  balance leastconn
  server database1 192.168.50.10:1433 check slowstart 60s
```

The server will progressively accept more and more connections during this time.

Weighted leastconn algorithm

While the purpose of the leastconn algorithm is to divide traffic so that busy servers get fewer requests, its only metric for evaluating how busy is the number of connections a server is currently servicing. Other factors like RAM and CPU aren't factored into the equation. So, if an older, slower server has fewer connections than other machines, but those connections happen to be maxing out its resources, the load balancer will still happily send new requests to it because it has the fewest connections.

To mitigate this, give each server a `weight` to inform HAProxy how much load a server is able to handle. Let's revisit our database example, but now assume that oldserver is an old server that's been brought out of retirement to work as a database replica. We will only send 1/5 of the traffic to it because it has less powerful hardware. The number of connections it's receiving will also be considered.

```
frontend my_readonly_database
  mode tcp
  bind *:1433
  default_backend database_replicas
```

```
backend database_replicas
  mode tcp
  balance leastconn
  server newserver 192.168.50.15:1433 weight 4
  server oldserver 192.168.50.16:1433 weight 1
```

Before, I briefly mentioned that it's important to have enough servers in a `backend` to handle all of the traffic if one or two servers fail. This is especially true when you have less capable servers in the mix. Be sure to have enough capacity to survive random server failures.

Hash URI algorithm

Let's suppose that the website you're load balancing has a cache, such as Varnish, in front of it. So if the client requests http://mysite.com/cats.jpg, the request will go to the cache first to see if cats.jpg is there. If it is, which is known as a cache hit, the file can be returned without having to bother the backend Web server at all. This can potentially improve the speed of your site because, in addition to the image being returned faster because it was served by a cache that is optimized to return static content faster than a Web server can, the Web server also gets a boost because it doesn't have to handle as many requests.

Now let's suppose that, to improve scalability, you have two caches. If we use roundrobin or leastconn load balancing, then requests for cats.jpg will be spread over all of the backend cache servers more or less equally, reducing the chances of getting a cache hit. Each time, the cache handling the request will have to fetch the file from the Web server if it doesn't already have it. If, instead, all requests for cats.jpg had gone to, say, cache #1, then it would only have to be fetched the first time someone asked for it. In other words, our cache hit rate would go up.

The hash URI load-balancing algorithm looks at the path of the URL being requested, which includes everything after the first forward slash and before the first question mark, such as cats.jpg in the URL http://mysite.com/cats.jpg, and sends identical requests to the same backend server. To do this, HAProxy stores a hash of the URL along with the ID of the server that responded to that request last time. In the following example, we have two cache servers that are load balanced using `balance uri`.

```
backend cache_servers
  balance uri
  server cache1 192.168.50.20:80
  server cache2 192.168.50.21:80
```

Note that in this configuration, our cache servers sit betwen HAProxy and your Web servers. You can also have more requests go to a certain cache if it's a more powerful machine. Give the `server` a `weight`. In the next snippet, twice as many requests will be forwarded to the cache2 server compared to cache1.

```
backend cache_servers
  balance uri
  server cache1 192.168.50.20:80 weight 1
  server cache2 192.168.50.21:80 weight 2
```

I mentioned that the part of the URL that HAProxy looks at is between the first forward slash and the first question mark. But what if the URL parameters matter? Take, for instance, the URI http://mywebsite.com/cats.jpg?width=400&height=200. What if the width and height parameters here dynamically changed the image that should be fetched? In that case, we can add the `whole` parameter to specify that we want to have HAProxy hash the rest of the URI past the question mark.

```
balance uri whole
```

Now HAProxy will try to match on cats.jpg?width=400&height=200 and we'll be able to direct future requests for that file to a single server.

First available algorithm

Servers aren't cheap. Even virtual servers cost money to operate for reasons like electricity usage and software licensing. That's why it might make sense to disable servers when not needed. HAProxy can accommodate this with its first available load-balancing algorithm. When set in a `backend` group of servers, all traffic will be directed to a single `server` until its maximum number of connections is reached. Then the extra traffic begins to flow to the next `server` in the lineup. This allows us to use the fewest servers and keep our costs down.

The following snippet uses `balance first` to direct traffic to the first server, from top to bottom, that has available connection slots. When its `maxconn` limit is reached, traffic will begin to flow to the next server. It is important to set the `maxconn` parameter on the `server` directive or else the first server would accept as many connections as HAProxy can throw at it, while the others wouldn't get any.

```
backend webservers
  balance first
  server web1 192.168.50.10:80 maxconn 30
  server web2 192.168.50.11:80 maxconn 30
  server web3 192.168.50.12:80 maxconn 30
```

The `maxconn` parameter is valuable even if you're not using first available load balancing. It determines how many connections to send to a backend server before either sending the request to another available server or queuing connections until a server becomes available. HAProxy is pretty good at queuing many thousands of connections and doling them out to servers only when the servers are ready to receive them.

If your backend servers have a quick response time, it won't take long for them to cycle through the entire queue even though they're processing small batches of requests at a time. Also, if a server is being sluggish about freeing up connection slots, HAProxy can send the request to another server instead. If that connection had been queued in the Web server instead, then there'd be nowhere else it could go. The total number of connections that HAProxy will accept is set by the `maxconn` setting in the `global` section. It defaults to 2000.

Summary

In this chapter, we learned that when it comes to choosing how to distribute traffic to your backend servers, you've got plenty of options. The roundrobin algorithm is simple to understand and easy to predict. It routes traffic to servers in a rotation so that each one gets an equal amount. We can tip the scales more towards some servers by assigning a higher `weight` to them.

The leastconn algorithm is a good choice for servers that may hold onto connections longer, such as database instances. It chooses which server to forward a request to based on how many active connections each one is already processing. This means we won't overload any particular machine. Like roundrobin, we can add a `weight` to our servers to send a higher or lower proportion of traffic to them.

If we're querying caches, it might make sense to use the hash URI algorithm so that requests for the same file are always sent to the same place. This keeps our cache hit rate high, which improves responsiveness and reduces load on our Web servers.

The first available algorithm can help us keep our operating costs low since it uses each server to its max before utilizing another. When servers aren't used, they could be disabled.

Chapter 5

Directing Traffic

HAProxy can load balance databases, mail servers and other services that don't use the HTTP protocol. However, it has extra features for handling Web traffic. In particular, it can inspect each HTTP request and check whether they match rules that we've set up. If they do, the request can be forwarded to a specific `backend` of our choosing. For example, we could send all requests for static images to one group of servers. Other requests would go to a different group. That way, some servers could focus on generating dynamic content while others focus on only serving content that never changes.

In this chapter, we will cover the following topics:

- Content switching based on the URL requested
- Content switching based on URL parameters
- Content switching based on HTTP headers
- Redirecting to another website
- Redirecting based on geolocation

Content switching on the URL path

Content switching refers to choosing a specific `backend` to handle a request when it matches some criteria. As you may recall, we can define this criteria with an `acl` directive. In this section, we'll look at some ACLs that inspect the request's URL path. Reasons why you might want to do this include:

- making different web applications running on different servers, perhaps built using different technology stacks, seem like they are part of a single, cohesive website. For example requests for /cart might be processed by one group of servers while other requests go to another.

- forwarding API calls, such as those that have a URL beginning with /api, to dedicated servers.

- serving dynamically generated files from dedicated servers while serving static images, JavaScript and CSS files from another so that we can optimize more effectively.

The following table lists the fetch methods that relate to inspecting parts of a URL's path:

Fetch method	What it does
path	exact string match
path_beg	URL begins with string
path_dir	subdirectory match
path_end	suffix match
path_len	length match
path_reg	regex match
path_sub	substring match

Use these methods to define the criteria of an `acl`. Then, use the `use_backend` directive to forward the request to the given `backend` if that ACL returns true. In the following example, we define an `acl` called is_api that checks if the URL begins with /api. If it does, we send it to the apiservers `backend` pool of servers. Otherwise, we send it to the webservers `backend`, as defined by our `default_backend` directive. We include the `-i` flag so that the matching is case-insensitive. Otherwise, /api would match but /API would not.

```
frontend mywebsite
  bind *:80
```

```
  acl is_api path_beg -i /api
  use_backend apiservers if is_api
  default_backend webservers

backend apiservers
   server api1 192.168.50.15:80
   server api2 192.168.50.16:80

backend webservers
   server web1 192.168.50.10:80
   server web2 192.168.50.11:80
```

Let's look at some other examples. Each of these `acl` directives would be placed in a `frontend` section and paired with a `use_backend`. The following would only match the exact URL http://mysite.com/super_sale/january/15:

```
acl jansale path -i /super_sale/january/15
```

Here we match if the URL begins with /cart, such as http://mysite.com/cart/items:

```
acl iscart path_beg -i /cart
```

In the next example, we match if the URL is a subdirectory of shirts, such as http://mysite.com/shirts/blue:

```
acl isshirts path_dir -i /shirts
```

In the next example, we match if the URL ends with .jpg or .png, such as http://mysite.com/shirts/redshirt.jpg:

```
acl isimage path_end -i .jpg .png
```

We can match if the URL is a given length. The following will match if the URL path, including the first forward slash, is exactly four characters long, such as http://mysite.com/123:

```
acl exactlyfour path_len 4
```

We can also use a comparison operator to check if the length of the path is greater-than (gt), greater-than-or-equal-to (ge), less-than (lt), or less-than-or-equal-to (le) a number. The following will match if the URL is longer than four characters, matching http://mysite.com/1234:

```
acl longerthan4 path_len gt 4
```

We can also match against a regular expression. The following will match any path ending with png, jpg, jpeg or gif, such as http://mysite.com/cats.gif.

```
acl isimage path_reg (png|jpg|jpeg|gif)$
```

The following will match if the URL contains the substring sale, such as http://mysite.com/on-sale/shirts:

```
acl onsale path_sub -i sale
```

Note that if you define more than one `acl`, then they'll be parsed in the same order as you've defined your `use_backend` statements. In the following snippet, we first check if the URL is for our old, deprecated API, /api/v1, and then if it is for our current API, /api/v2. Last, we fall back to our default webservers `backend`. The order of the `acl` directives doesn't matter, only the order of the `use_backend` statements.

```
frontend mywebsite
  bind *:80
  acl isoldapi path_beg -i /api/v1
  acl iscurrentapi path_beg -i /api/v2
  use_backend oldapiservers if isoldapi
  use_backend apiservers if iscurrentapi
  default_backend webservers
```

Content switching on a URL parameter

We can send traffic to a specific `backend` if we see a particular parameter in the URL. Let's suppose that we wanted to always be directed to the west_coast_servers backend when we see a parameter named region set to west in the URL. This might be useful for debugging that group of servers. Use the `url_param` fetch method to get the value of a URL parameter.

In this snippet, we check whether the request's URL has a region parameter set to west, such as http://mysite.com/?region=west. The `-m str` operator means that we want an exact string match.

```
frontend mywebsite
  bind *:80
  acl iswest url_param(region) -m str west
  use_backend west_coast_servers if iswest
  default_backend webservers
```

This rule will not match if the capitalization is different. For example, the region parameter in the URL http://mysite.com/?region=West begins with a capital letter and so would not match our rule. To fix this, add the `-i` switch so that matching is case-insensitive.

```
acl iswest url_param(region) -i -m str west
```

If you'd like to match serveral possible strings, then simply separate the values with spaces. For example, to match the strings west, westcoast or wc we would set our `acl` to:

```
acl iswest url_param(region) -i -m str west westcoast wc
```

Maybe, instead of looking for an exact value, you'd like to check for the existence of a parameter named west and its value doesn't matter. For this, use the `-m reg` operator to specify a regular expression of .+, which will match any value, such as http://mysite.com/?west=1 or http://mysite.com/?west=yadayada.

```
acl iswest url_param(west) -m reg .+
```

Content switching on an HTTP header

When deciding which `backend` to send a client to, we can also consider the HTTP headers present in their request. Suppose we wanted to know whether the client is using a mobile phone to access our site. The User-Agent header contains text that'll help us guess which type of device they're using. It might look like this for an iPhone user:

> User-Agent: Mozilla/5.0 (iPhone; U; CPU iPhone OS 4_0 like Mac OS X; en-us) AppleWebKit/532.9 (KHTML, like Gecko) Version/4.0.5 Mobile/8A293 Safari/6531.22.7

Similarly, when the client is using an Android device, the text Android will be present in the User-Agent text. With HAProxy, we can use the `req.hdr` fetch method to get the value of any HTTP request header. The following examples uses a regular expression to check whether the User-Agent header contains the words Android or iPhone. The -i switch makes the search case-insensitive. Using this rule, we can send mobile phone browser traffic to our mobileservers `backend`. All other traffic will go to the webservers `backend`.

```
frontend mysite
  bind *:80
  acl ismobile req.hdr(User-Agent) -i -m reg (android|iphone)
  use_backend mobileservers if ismobile
  default_backend webservers
```

To test this, you can use Google Chrome's Developer Tools, which have a built-in device emulator.

Another use for `req.hdr` is to direct traffic to a different `backend` based on the Host header. The Host contains the website name that the client typed into their browser's address bar. Suppose we manage several shoe store websites, but want them to be proxied through the same `frontend`. The load balancer will be in charge of directing the request to the correct `backend` based on the Host that the client requested.

In the following example, we send requests for www.cheapshoes.com to the cheapshoesservers `backend` and requests for www.expensiveshoes.com to the expensiveshoesservers `backend`.

Figure 5.1: Chrome Device Emulator

```
frontend allmyshoestores
  bind *:80
  acl ischeapshoes req.hdr(Host) -i -m str www.cheapshoes.com
  acl isexpensiveshoes req.hdr(Host) -i -m str www.expensiveshoes.com
  use_backend cheapshoesservers if ischeapshoes
  use_backend expensiveshoesservers if isexpensiveshoes
```

To match more than one Host, separate them with spaces. So, to match cheapshoes.com and www.cheapshoes.com, we could use the following:

```
acl ischeapshoes req.hdr(Host) -i -m str cheapshoes.com www.cheapshoes.com
```

Redirecting to another URL

Content switching is the appropriate technique when we want portions of a website to be processed by different backend servers. Sometimes though, we need to visibly redirect the client to another site. Reasons to do this include:

- the domain name of your website has changed.

- to redirect from misspelled versions of your website to the correct spelling.

- to redirect to a canonical name of your website, such as from www.mysite.com to mysite.com

Adding a `redirect prefix` directive to a `frontend` tells HAProxy to intercept a request and forward it to another URL. Suppose we changed the name of our website from prettygoodshoes.com to amazingshoes.com and wanted clients who visit the old site to be sent to the new one. The following examples illustrates how this could be done using `redirect prefix`. Note that we're adding an `acl` that uses the `req.hdr(Host)` fetch method to get the value of the Host HTTP header and check if it's set to the name of our old site.

```
frontend mywebsite
  bind *:80
  default_backend webservers
  acl wantsprettygoodshoes req.hdr(Host) -i -m str prettygoodshoes.com
  redirect prefix http://amazingshoes.com if wantsprettygoodshoes
```

The nice thing about `redirect prefix` is that it will carry over the entire URL path to the domain that you redirect to. For example, http://prettygoodshoes.com/kids/boots.html would be forwarded to http://amazingshoes.com/kids/boots.html. URL parameters will carry over too, so http://prettygoodshoes.com/search/?color=blue would be forwarded to http://amazingshoes.com/search/?color=blue. However, if you prefer, you can remove the URL parameters by adding the `drop-query` parameter. The following snippet would strip off any URL query parameters before forwarding to amazingshoes.com.

```
redirect prefix http://amazingshoes.com drop-query if wantsprettygoodshoes
```

We can also control the type of redirect that's performed by adding the `code` parameter. By default, HAProxy uses an HTTP response code 302, but we can choose any of the following:

Code	Meaning
301	The current and all future requests should use the new URL.
302	The current request should be forwarded to the new URL. Future requests should use the original URL.

Code	Meaning
303	The current request should be forwarded to the new URL, but as a GET. For example, if a a client sends a POST request to a form that submits a shopping cart, they could be redirected to another page that shows details of the purchase, but using a GET request. This page can be bookmarked, refreshed, etc. without resubmitting the form. This is available in HTTP/1.1.
307	The current request should be forwarded to the new URL, but do not change the HTTP verb used. For example, if POST was used before, use POST again. Future requests should use the original URL. This is available in HTTP/1.1.
308	The current and all future requests should use the new URL. Do not change the HTTP verb used. For example, if POST was used before, use POST again. This is available in HTTP/1.1.

Here's an example that uses `code 301` instead:

`redirect prefix http://amazingshoes.com code 301 if wantsprettygoodshoes`

We can also direct clients to our new website's root URL no matter which page they were trying to access on the old site. Simply use `redirect location` instead of `redirect prefix` and the entire URL will be replaced with the new URL that we specify. The following example would direct http://prettygoodshoes.com/kids/boots?color=blue to http://amazingshoes.com:

`redirect location http://amazingshoes.com if wantsprettygoodshoes`

When HAProxy responds with a redirect status code like this, the client's browser will reissue its request to the new destination. It probably goes without saying, but you will have to configure HAProxy to accept requests for this IP address too if you plan on load balancing it.

Redirecting based on geolocation

Geolocation, for our purposes, means identifying a client's geographical location by their IP address. HAProxy has support for mapping IP address ranges to country

CHAPTER 5. DIRECTING TRAFFIC

codes, which opens the door to redirecting the client to a server that's closest to them. In this scenario, you would likely want to have instances of HAProxy running on multiple servers in different regions of the world, rather than trying to route requests through a single, central instance.

To make geolocation possible, we need a database that contains the IP address-to-region mappings. MaxMind offers a free geolocation database called GeoLite. In your browser, navigate to http://dev.maxmind.com/geoip/legacy/geolite and download the GeoLite Country CSV file. The file will be called GeoIPCountryCSV.zip. After unzipping it, you will see that it contains a CSV file that lists the IP ranges used by different countries. Here's a sample of its contents:

```
"2.0.0.0","2.0.0.0","33554432","33554432","GB","United Kingdom"
"2.0.0.1","2.15.255.255","33554433","34603007","FR","France"
"2.16.0.0","2.16.5.255","34603008","34604543","EU","Europe"
"2.16.6.0","2.16.7.255","34604544","34605055","DE","Germany"
```

Each line has six fields, but we only need the first, second and fifth. We want it to look like this:

```
"2.0.0.0","2.0.0.0","GB"
"2.0.0.1","2.15.255.255","FR"
"2.16.0.0","2.16.5.255","EU"
"2.16.6.0","2.16.7.255","DE"
```

Use the Linux `cut` command to format the file the way we want. The -d parameter sets the delimiter to a comma and the -f parameter selects the fields that we want to keep. Send the output of this command to a text file called geo_ip.txt.

```
~$ cut -d, -f1,2,5 GeoIPCountryWhois.csv > geo_ip.txt
```

Or, if you're editing this file on Windows, you can use this slightly more verbose Powershell command:

```
Import-Csv ./GeoIPCountryWhois.csv -Header 1,2,3,4,5,6 |
   Select "1","2","5" | ConvertTo-Csv -NoTypeInformation |
   Select-Object -Skip 1 | Set-Content geo_ip.txt
```

Next, we want to change the format of the file so that instead of having a beginning and ending IP address for each country such as "2.0.0.1","2.15.255.255","FR", we have one IP address with a CIDR notation to denote the range, such as 2.0.0.1/32 "FR". There's a tool that will do this for us, called iprange, that is included in the HAProxy source code.

Download the HAProxy 1.6 source code from http://www.haproxy.org. Extract the files from the haproxy-1.6.5.tar.gz tarball and you'll find iprange.c and a Makefile in the contrib/iprange folder. Compile the iprange tool by navigating into this folder and calling the `make` command.

```
~$ cd haproxy-1.6.6/contrib/iprange
~$ make
```

This will compile the iprange.c file into the iprange executable. We can now use it to update our geo_ip.txt file to the desired format. Copy geo_ip.txt to the iprange folder and execute `iprange` like so:

```
~$ cat geo_ip.txt | ./iprange > geolocation.txt
```

You should now have a file called geolocation.txt that contains IP ranges with country codes.

```
2.0.0.1/32 "FR"
2.0.0.2/31 "FR"
2.0.0.4/30 "FR"
2.0.0.8/29 "FR"
```

Copy the geolocation.txt file to the /etc/haproxy directory on the machine where HAProxy is installed. Then update HAProxy's configuration file, /etc/haproxy/haproxy.cfg, to use the `map_ip` fetch method to get the country code that's mapped to the client's IP address. The `map_ip` method takes a path to a file that contains key-value pairs. In the following example, we use `map_ip` to set the value of an HTTP request header called X-Country to the client's corresponding country code. Be careful not to have any spaces between `src,` and `map_ip`.

```
frontend mywebsite
  bind *:80
  default_backend webservers
  http-request set-header X-Country
    %[src,map_ip(/etc/haproxy/geolocation.txt)]
```

Note that if your source IP is an internal IP address, which is likely during testing, you will have to update the geolocation.txt file so that it includes that range too. Using a network analyzer like Wireshark or tcpdump, you should see the new header in the HTTP request after it's forwarded to the backend server. A tcpdump command to see incoming GET requests and their headers is:

```
~$ sudo tcpdump -i eth0 -s 0 -A
    'tcp[((tcp[12:1] & 0xf0) >> 2):4] = 0x47455420'
```

You should see the X-Country header with a value like X-Country: "US".

Once we have the client's country code, we can redirect them to a geographically close server. First, to find out if the client is in the United States, let's create an `acl` that compares the X-Country header with the value US. Then, we'll use `redirect location` to send them to a website specific to that region, such as us.mywebsite.com.

```
frontend mywebsite
  bind *:80
  http-request set-header X-Country
    %[src,map_ip(/etc/haproxy/geolocation.txt)]
  acl is-unitedstates req.hdr(X-Country) -m sub -i US
  redirect location http://us.mywebsite.com if is-unitedstates
  default_backend webservers
```

All that's left to do is set up an instance of HAProxy on a server in the United States that has a `frontend` bound to the IP address that us.mywebsite.com resolves to.

Summary

In this chapter, we learned how to use content switching to send traffic to a specific `backend` pool of servers based on an `acl`. The criteria used might include text that we find in the URL, the values of URL parameters or the values of HTTP request headers.

We also saw how to redirect to a different website by using the `redirect location` and `redirect prefix` directives. We can even base our redirection on the client's geographic location so that they're sent to the server that's closest to them. MaxMind offers a free geolocation database and we can use a tool called iprange from the HAProxy source code to parse it into the format we need.

Chapter 6

Detecting and Reacting to Failure

It's important to detect failed machines early and remove them from our server pool. If clients are allowed to be routed to unreachable or failed servers, then they might see error messages or not get through at all. HAProxy is able to monitor our servers with periodic health checks and automatically remove unhealthy nodes. Traffic will only be sent to machines that are up.

In this chapter, we will cover the following topics:

- Enabling TCP-based health checks
- Using HTTP-based checks for services communicating over HTTP
- Configuring which responses count as successful checks
- Having a server depend on the health of another
- Setting a backup server
- Failing over when there aren't enough servers left
- Observing real traffic for errors

TCP-based health checks

When, for whatever reason, we can't connect to a backend server, we want to know about it as soon as possible. The sooner we know, the sooner we can direct traffic elsewhere. HAProxy can keep tabs on whether a server is up through periodic attempts to connect to its IP address and port. In the next snippet, we enable health checking by adding the `check` parameter to the web1 `server` directive. If a TCP connection can be made to that server's listening port, in this case port 80, then the check passes.

```
frontend mywebsite
  bind *:80
  default_backend webservers

backend webservers
  balance roundrobin
  server web1 192.168.50.10:80 check
```

When HAProxy can't connect to a server anymore, it will remove it from the load-balancing rotation and traffic will not be sent to it. HAProxy will continue to send health checks though, attempting to connect to the IP and port, so that it knows when the server has come back online. When that happens, traffic will resume flowing to it. If all servers in a `backend` fail, HAProxy will respond to the client with HTTP 503 Service Unavailable.

Health checks are performed every two seconds, but you can change that with the `inter` parameter. The interval can be set in days (d), hours (h), minutes (m), seconds (s), milliseconds (ms), or microseconds (us). In the following example we perform a health check every ten seconds.

```
server web1 192.168.50.10:80 check inter 10s
```

When a server fails a health check, it is not removed from the rotation immediately. A server must fail three consecutive checks before it is considered down. This protects us from momentary losses in connectivity that might take the server offline unnecessarily. We can change this threshold with the `fall` parameter. In the following example the server can fail only two health checks before being declared unreachable.

```
server web1 192.168.50.10:80 check inter 10s fall 2
```

Keep in mind that the total amount of time that a client will be sent to a failed server is determined by multiplying the interval of the checks by the threshold set by the `fall` parameter. So, if our checks occur every ten seconds and we require two failed checks, then the maximum amount of time that a client could be sent to a failed server would be 20 seconds. In general, you don't want the interval to be too large because then users may be directed to a dead server longer than necessary. On the other hand, you don't want to set the interval so small that the server is bombarded with health checks.

We can also control the number of times that a server must report as being healthy before being put back into the rotation. It defaults to two, but we can change it with the `rise` parameter. The next example declares that the server must have five successful health checks before being considered truly recovered.

```
server web1 192.168.50.10:80 check inter 10s fall 2 rise 5
```

One tactic is to fail fast and recover slow, meaning take a server out of the rotation soon after you detect a problem and then require a higher number of successful health checks before putting it back into action. This gives us the highest level of confidence that our machines are stable.

You can also change how often checks are sent to a down server. For example, once a server is unreachable, you might think Why send constant checks to a server that isn't likely to recover any time soon?. In that case, you might only want to check it every two minutes. For this, add the `downinter` parameter like so:

```
server web1 192.168.50.10:80 check downinter 2m
```

By default, HAProxy tries to connect to the same IP and port that's set for the `server` directive. However, if we wanted, we could check a completely different port or IP address by setting the `addr` and `port` parameters.

```
server web1 192.168.50.10:80 check addr 192.168.50.11 port 81
```

You might do this if a service is listening at that address that can perform complex checks against your server.

HTTP-based health checks

A drawback of enabling health checks with the `check` parameter is that success is measured only by the ability to make a TCP connection to the backend sever's IP address and port. So, even if the Web server begins responding with HTTP 500 Internal Server Error, the checks will still pass as long as a connection can be made. So, clients might be sent to webpages that are displaying errors. If we're using `mode http`, we can make our health checks a little smarter: We can have them look for a successful HTTP response. Basically, any response in the 2xx and 3xx range is good. To use this feature, add the `option httpchk` directive to the `backend`.

```
backend webservers
  mode http
  balance roundrobin
  server web1 192.168.50.10:80 check
  option httpchk
```

When we pair `option httpchk` with the `server` directive's `check` parameter, HAProxy regularly sends HTTP requests to the servers and stops sending clients to any that do not send back a successful HTTP response. Instead of sending a GET, it uses the HTTP OPTIONS method. The OPTIONS method is a lightweight request that asks which HTTP methods the server accepts. Then, a server might respond that it accepts GET, POST, PUT and OPTIONS methods for instance. The small size of the response makes it well suited for a health check.

Beware that some servers, such as NGINX, don't respond to the OPTIONS method and instead return an HTTP 405 Method Not Allowed response. In that case, we can specify another method to use for the health checks, along with the path on the server to test. In the following example, we've updated the `option httpchk` directive to use the HEAD method and to target the path /testpage.

```
backend webservers
  mode http
  balance roundrobin
  server web1 192.168.50.10:80 check
  option httpchk HEAD /testpage
```

Some servers require that we send a valid Host header with our request. To do so, add it to the end of the `option httpchk` parameter like so:

```
option httpchk HEAD /testpage HTTP/1.1\r\nHost:\ mywebsite.com
```

Now, the server will receive health checks that look like this:

```
HEAD /testpage HTTP/1.1
Host: mywebsite.com
```

Expecting specific responses

As we've seen, when we use the `option httpchk` directive, HAProxy continually sends HTTP requests to a backend server to verify that it's healthy. It will consider any response status code that's in the 2xx or 3xx range as a passing check. We can also tell HAProxy to look for a specific status code by setting the `status` parameter on the `http-check expect` directive. In the following snippet, we expect to only receive a status of 200 OK.

```
backend webservers
  mode http
  balance roundrobin
  server web1 192.168.50.10:80 check
  server web2 192.168.50.11:80 check
  option httpchk HEAD /testpage
  http-check expect status 200
```

The `http-check expect` directive can do more than this, though. First off, if we wanted to consider any status code in the 2xx range, not just 200, as a passing check, but all others as failures, we could set the `rstatus` parameter to a regular expression. The next snippet checks whether the returned status code is a 2 followed by two more numbers.

```
http-check expect rstatus ^2(\d){2}$
```

We can also check for certain text in the body of the response. For this to work, we'll need to use an HTTP GET so that the server returns a body. In the next snippet, we use the `rstring` parameter to set a regular expression that will check for the presence of the word success anywhere in the body of the response. If it's missing, the check will fail and the server will eventually be removed from the load-balancing rotation.

```
option httpchk GET /testpage
http-check expect rstring success
```

Our webserver can have sophisticated, internal checks that culminate in returning a status code or string of text to the tested webpage. For example, the website could check that it is able to communicate with other services and databases and then return a string of success if everything works. If we wanted to do maintenance on a server, we could fail a check on purpose to take the server offline. However, HAProxy gives us a directive for this exact purpose. When we use `http-check disable-on-404`, the server will be disabled if it sends 404 Not Found in response to a health check.

```
option httpchk HEAD /testpage
http-check disable-on-404
```

To enable the server again, simply send a 200 OK response.

Relying on the status of another server

Sometimes, we may want to report a `server` as down if a service that it depends on is down. Consider a hotel reservation service that must query a database to see how many rooms are still available. If the service cannot reach the database, we might want to disable it until the database becomes available again. That way, we are safeguarded against double-booking a room. The rest of the hotel's website would remain functional, even though its reservation system was offline. The alternative is to allow the possibility that two customers might book the same room, which would mean requiring one of them cancel later on, which isn't great customer service. Or, worse, our reservation service might get errors when a customer tried to book a room.

We can have a `server` track the health of another `server`. In the following snippet, reservations_service depends on the health of databases/db1. If db1 goes down, reservations_service will also report as down. When db1 comes back online, reservations_service will also come back up. Keep in mind that if all of the servers in our reservations_service `backend` report as down, HAProxy will return a 503 Service Unavailable response. Our website must be prepared for this contingency.

```
backend reservations_service
  mode http
  server rs1 192.168.50.10:80 track databases/db1

backend databases
  mode tcp
  server db1 192.168.60.10:1433 check
```

We can have a server track another server which, in turn, tracks another server. However, at the end of the line there must be a `server` with a `check` parameter. If a `server` uses the `track` parameter, it cannot use the `check` parameter too.

While `track` is good for taking a single `server` offline if another service it depends on is down, we can also perform a similar check from within a `frontend`. We can use the `srv_is_up` fetch method to check whether a particular `server` is down and if it is, switch to using a completely different `backend` pool of servers. In the following example, our website fails over to another reservation system if the database that its primary system relies on is offline.

```
frontend mywebsite
  bind *:80
  acl primarydbonline srv_is_up(primary_database/db1)
  use_backend primary_service if primarydbonline
  default_backend backup_service

backend primary_service
  mode http
  server primary1 192.168.50.10:80 check

backend backup_service
  mode http
  server backup1 192.168.50.20:80 check

backend primary_database
  mode tcp
  server db1 192.168.60.10:1433 check
```

In this case, we are not using the `track` parameter. The mywebsite `frontend` is responsible for checking whether the database is online and choosing the corresponding backend.

Setting a backup server

Designating a `server` as a `backup` means that it will not be used unless all other servers in the same `backend` are unavailable. This effectively sets up an active-passive configuration that's useful for situations where only one server can be turned on at a time. For example, some credit card processors will give you a backup IP address to use in case a primary fails, but you are not allowed to send credit card authorization requests to both at the same time.

In the following example, we set service2 as our `backup` server. It will only be used if service1 can't be reached.

```
backend webservice
   server service1 192.168.50.10:80 check
   server service2 192.168.50.11:80 check backup
```

We can set more than one backup server. However, ordinarily, if all primary servers fail only the first backup will be used. By adding the `option allbackups` directive, multiple backups will be brought online at the same time and using the same load balancing algorithm as the regular servers. In the following example, if both service1 and service2 go offline, service3 and service4 will take over.

```
backend webservice
   balance roundrobin
   server service1 192.168.50.10:80 check
   server service2 192.168.50.11:80 check
   server service3 192.168.50.12:80 check backup
   server service4 192.168.50.13:80 check backup
   option allbackups
```

When the original servers comes back up, traffic will flow to them again while the backup servers are taken offline. Note that the backups won't be activated until all of the regular servers fail.

Failing over when not enough servers are left

When planning how many servers are needed to handle the average amount of traffic your website or service receives, you'll find that there is a minimum number needed to prevent overwhelming your machines. Depending on the amount of traffic, one or two servers might be enough or you might need ten. Whatever the number is, there's a line you must draw at which if a certain number of your servers fail, the rest won't be enough to handle the traffic on their own. At that point, the traffic begins to overload the remaining machines until they too fail.

With HAProxy, we can use the `nbsrv` fetch method to check how many servers are currently up in a `backend`. If that number is less than our minimum, we can fail over to a completely different `backend` pool of servers. In the following snippet, we've defined an `acl` called less_than_three that uses the `nbsrv` fetch method to check whether the primaryservers `backend` has less than three servers that are passing their health checks. If so, we switch to using the backupservers `backend`. When enough servers become healthy again in our primaryservers `backend`, traffic will be routed there again.

```
frontend mywebsite
  bind *:80
  acl less_than_three nbsrv(primaryservers) lt 3
  use_backend backupservers if less_than_three
  default_backend primaryservers

backend primaryservers
  balance roundrobin
    server web1 192.168.50.10:80 check
    server web2 192.168.50.11:80 check
    server web3 192.168.50.12:80 check

backend backupservers
  balance roundrobin
    server web4 192.168.60.10:80 check
    server web5 192.168.60.11:80 check
    server web6 192.168.60.12:80 check
```

Not only does this solution work well for failing over when we don't have enough capacity to handle the incoming trafifc, it's also good for recovering from a failure of

Observing all requests for errors

Let's say that you've set up HAProxy as a reverse proxy in front of a database. If that database consistently receives requests throughout the day, you might think to yourself, With this regular traffic, why do I also need to send these constant TCP health checks? Can't I just monitor the regular traffic for errors?. It turns out, you can. By adding an `observe layer4` parameter to our `server` directives, HAProxy will monitor for a failed connection from any client, not just failed connections from our regular health checks. We can use this feature for any `backend` that's using `mode tcp`.

In the following example, we monitor all connections to the db1 server for errors. If we see three consecutive failed connections, we will take the server offline just like we would if we'd had three failed health checks.

```
backend msql_databases
  mode tcp
  balance roundrobin
  server db1 192.168.50.20:3306 check fall 3  inter 2m  observe layer4
    error-limit 1
  server db2 192.168.50.21:3306 check backup
```

We've set the db1 server's interval at which it sends health checks to every two minutes because, when we're checking the existing traffic for connection errors, we don't need to send our own health checks as often. The `fall` parameter means that we can only have three failed checks before stopping traffic from being routed to that server.

Next, we've added an `observe layer4` parameter that tells HAProxy to monitor all TCP connections to the server. To set the number of bad connection we'll allow before counting it as a failed health check, we've set an `error-limit` parameter on the `server` directive. In this case, we've set `error-limit` to 1 so that every failed connection counts as a failed health check. If this number were higher, we'd have to see more failed connections from clients before HAProxy would increment the failed health check count.

This technique works well when we have consistent traffic to our servers. It lets us have fewer regular health checks and instead rely on checking actual traffic for errors. It also works when using `mode http`, in which case we can use `observe layer7` to monitor HTTP traffic. If a client receives a 503 Server Error when accessing any page, HAProxy will consider it a failed health check.

In the following example, if web1 sees three consecutive failed checks, which we increment whenever a client gets a server error, we mark the server as down.

```
backend webservers
  mode http
  balance roundrobin
  server web1 192.168.50.10:80 check fall 3  inter 2m
    observe layer7  error-limit 1
  server web2 192.168.50.11:80 check backup
```

After a server has been taken offline, it can only be brought back after it has had enough passing health checks. At this point, we'll have to wait for HAProxy's traditional checks to happen. We've set the interval of those checks to be two minutes apart. So, beware that recovery will take longer. Also note that the traditional checks will continue to target the root URL, or whichever URL we've set with an `option httpchk` directive. That URL may not be getting server errors and may perceive the sever as healthy even if other pages are failing.

Monitoring for server downtime

HAProxy distributes traffic to each server in a `backend` according to the load-balancing algorithm that we've chosen. When one of those servers stops responding to our health checks, HAProxy stops sending traffic to it. That means our users are only sent to working servers and our websites and services will remain highly available. However, it's not enough to just remove defective servers from the mix. We also want to know when a server has failed or, more importantly, if all of our servers have failed.

System monitoring tools like Nagios and PRTG can send us alerts as long as we can find a way to feed them the right information. The first way to do this is by having the monitoring tool send an HTTP GET request to the HAProxy Stats page, which can be returned in CSV format. Add a `stats enable` directive in the `defaults` section of your HAProxy configuration file to turn on this webpage.

```
defaults
  stats enable
```

Then, when you request the page /haproxy?stats;csv, you'll get a comma-separated list of information about your servers. This will include which ones are reporting as down. Here's a truncated example of what this data looks like. Notice the `status` field, which shows UP for each `server` and also the `backend` as a whole. The status will show DOWN when the server has failed its health checks.

```
pxname,svname,qcur,qmax,scur,smax,slim,stot,bin,bout,dreq,dresp,
ereq,econ,eresp,wretr,wredis,status...

mywebsite,FRONTEND,,,3,3,2000,3,0,0,0,0,0,,,,,OPEN...
webservers,web1,0,0,0,0,,0,0,0,,0,,0,0,0,0,UP...
webservers,BACKEND,0,0,0,0,200,0,0,0,0,0,,0,0,0,0,UP...
```

We can write a script that makes an HTTP request to the Stats page, parses the CSV data and feeds it to a sensor defined within our monitoring software. I won't go into much detail about the script itself. You can read more about some that others have written by following these links. The first uses ruby to fetch the Stats data and parse the results. The second uses Windows PowerShell.

- Nagios sensor: https://exchange.nagios.org/directory/Plugins/Network-Connections,-Stats-and-Bandwidth/HAProxy-check/details
- PRTG sensor: http://lazic.info/josip/post/monitor-haproxy-via-prtg

Another way to monitor the availability of your servers is to use a `monitor-uri` directive. It should specify a URL that you'd like to monitor, but that does not map back to any real webpage hosted by your Web server.

```
frontend mywebsite
  bind *:80
```

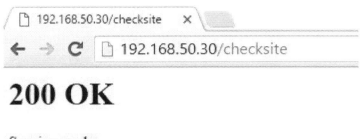

Figure 6.1: monitor-uri webpage

```
default_backend webservers
monitor-uri /checksite

backend webservers
  balance roundrobin
  server web1 192.168.50.31:80 check
```

Now, if you were to browse to that URL, such as http://192.168.50.30/checksite, you'd see a working webpage accompanied by a 200 Success HTTP response. The request is not forwarded to any backend server. HAProxy intercepts it and immediately returns that webpage.

In fact, even if you stopped your Web server, the URL will continue to return a successful response. So, a webpage that always returns a result that doesn't come from our backend servers. How is this useful? The trick is to have it return a failed response when we detect some condition. To do that, we'll specify an ACL that checks how many servers are up in a particular `backend`. If the count is down to zero, we use the `monitor fail` directive to return an HTTP 503 Service Unavailable response.

Here's an example that defines an ACL called zero_servers that uses the `nbsrv` fetch method to get the number of servers that are up in the given `backend`. If that number equals zero, the zero_servers ACL returns true. Then, the `monitor fail` directive updates the webpage to return the 503 status. When the servers come back online, the regular 200 OK webpage will be returned.

Figure 6.2: monitor-uri webpage showing failure

```
frontend mywebsite
  bind *:80
  default_backend webservers
  monitor-uri /checksite
  acl zero_servers nbsrv(webservers) eq 0
  monitor fail if zero_servers
```

You can also check for having less than a certain number of servers, if having fewer than that will not be enough to handle the traffic that your website or service receives. Simply update the ACL to use the less-than operator, lt, instead of equals, eq. In the following example, we check whether we have less than three healthy servers in the webservers backend. If so, the less_than_three ACL returns true and the monitor fail kicks in.

```
acl less_than_three nbsrv(webservers) lt 3
monitor fail if less_than_three
```

If you're using Nagios, a command to check that URL might look like this:

```
define command {
  command_name checksite
  command_line $USER1$/check_http -H $HOSTADDRESS$ --expect=200
    --url=/checksite
}
```

CHAPTER 6. DETECTING AND REACTING TO FAILURE 87

Monitoring a single URL for a successful response is a pretty straightforward way to get the status of your servers. However, if you want to get more detailed information, such as the current session rate at each server, then parsing the Stats page is a good option.

Emailing alerts

When it comes to being notified when something happens, such as when a server goes down, you're better off using a dedicated monitoring tool like Nagios to watch HAProxy. HAProxy's Stats webpage can be viewed in CSV format, which is easily parsed by these tools, or we can set up a `monitor-uri` directive. A good monitoring tool can:

- send an alert only once instead of over and over again
- alert you by email during the day and text messages at night
- know who to contact for different levels of escalation

Having said that, HAProxy comes with a built-in mechanism for sending emails when an event happens. It's primitive, but if you need simple email notifications without the frills, it does the job. To see how it works, we'll first need to set up an email server. If you already have one, you can skip this part.

We'll discuss how to install the Exim Message Transfer Agent (MTA). An MTA does not receive mail. It only sends it out, which is all we need for HAProxy to send email notifcations. Other programs, called Mail Delivery Agents (MDA) receive the mail on the recipient's end. MTAs send email over TCP port 25, which is a port that's often blocked by ISPs due to a long history of spamming. For that reason, we'll have Exim forward the message to Google's Gmail and then Gmail will send the message to its recipient. When Gmail relays mail on behalf of our email server, it is said to be acting as a smart host. Using a smart host gets around the limitation of using port 25 by sending the mail out over TCP port 587.

On the same machine where you have HAProxy installed, use your system's package manager to install exim4. Then call the `dpkg-reconfigure` command to configure it.

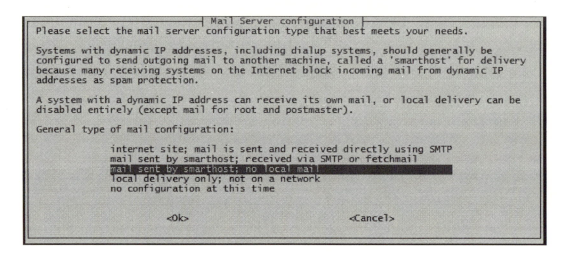

Figure 6.3: Exim wizard

```
~$ sudo apt update
~$ sudo apt install exim4 -y
~$ sudo dpkg-reconfigure exim4-config
```

That last command will display a wizard that will ask you questions about how to configure the mail server.

Answer it in this way:

- **General type of mail configuration:** mail sent by smarthost; no local mail

- **System mail name:** localhost

- **IP addresses to listen on for incoming SMTP connections:** 127.0.0.1; ::1

- **Other destinations for which mail is accepted:** empty

- **Visible domain name for local users:** localhost

- **IP address or host name of the outgoing smarthost:** smtp.gmail.com::587

- **Keep number of DNS queries minimal:** No

- **Split configuration into small files:** No

Next, edit the file /etc/exim4/passwd.client so that it contains your Gmail username and password. Gmail requires authentication before it will relay our mail. The passwd.client file should look like this:

```
*.google.com:myusername@gmail.com:mypassword
```

Restart the Exim service:

```
~$ sudo service exim4 restart
```

We can make sure that it started up okay with the following command:

```
~$ sudo service exim4 status
```

Then try sending an email message. In the following snippet, I use the `mail` command to send a message to a Hotmail account:

```
~$ echo "This is a test." | mail -s Test myotheremail@hotmail.com
```

If this message shows up in your inbox after a few moments, you know things are working. If not, re-run the wizard to correct any misconfigured settings.

Install HAProxy on the same machine if you haven't already done so and then edit your /etc/haproxy/haproxy.cfg file, adding a new section called `mailers`. This is where we'll define `mailer` directives that specify where our SMTP mail servers can be found. A `mailer` directive takes a label, like mymailserver, and the IP address, or DNS name, and port of the mail server.

An alert will be sent to each `mailer` in the list. We can now enable email alerts in our `defaults` section by referencing the `mailers` section with an `email-alert mailers` directive. Set `email-alert from` to the email address to show as the sender. Although when we're using a smart host it will use the smart host's email address for this. Set the `email-alert to` directive to the email address to send the alerts to. Finally, set `email-alert level` to the syslog level of events you'd like to be emailed about. A `level` of info will notify you when your servers fail and also when they come back online.

```
mailers mymailers
  mailer mymailserver 127.0.0.1:25

defaults
  mode http
  timeout connect 5s
  timeout client 120s
  timeout server 120s
  email-alert mailers mymailers
  email-alert from haproxy@mycompany.com
  email-alert to manager@mycompany.com
  email-alert level info

frontend mywebsite
  bind *:80
  default_backend webservers

backend webservers
  balance roundrobin
  server web1 192.168.50.31:80 check
```

The email message you'll receive will look like this:

> Server webservers/web1 is DOWN, reason: Layer4 connection problem, info: "Connection refused", check duration: 0ms. 0 active and 0 backup servers left. 0 sessions active, 0 requeued, 0 remaining in queue

When the server comes back up, you'll get another email like this:

> Server webservers/web1 is UP, reason: Layer4 check passed, check duration: 0ms. 1 active and 0 backup servers online. 0 sessions requeued, 0 total in queue

Summary

In this chapter, we learned that HAProxy can monitor our servers and take them out of the load-balancing rotation if it sees problems. This health-checking can occur at TCP layer 4 by simply adding a `check` parameter to our `server` directives. HAProxy will continuously attempt to connect to your server's IP address and port to detect failures. We can also perform health checks at layer 7 by complementing the `check` parameter with an `option httpchk` directive. HAProxy will send HTTP requests and expect to receive successful HTTP responses.

When using HTTP checks, we can set the URL that's monitored and the exact status code expected for a successful response. We can also disable the server if we get an HTTP 404 Not Found by using the `http-check disable-on-404` directive, which is great for gracefully draining traffic away from a server before doing maintenance on it.

When we've detected that a server has failed, traffic will not be sent to it. HAProxy offers features beyond this functionality though. We can set servers as backups so that they are only used if all others servers are unreachable. We can also, via fetch methods like `nbsrv`, specify how many servers must remain available to handle the traffic. If we lose more than that, we're able to fail over to another `backend`.

Health checks occur at regular intervals. However, when we consistently receive continuous traffic, why not watch that for errors too? Using `observe layer4` or `observe layer7` we can do just that. When clients start seeing problems, we'll be able to react faster without having to wait for a traditional health check.

We also saw how to monitor our servers with tools like Nagios. The stats page can be rendered in CSV format, which is easily parsed or we can set up a dedicated `monitor-uri` endpoint. Last, we learned how to enable email notification from HAProxy.

Chapter 7

Server Persistence

When a client makes a request to our website, HAProxy chooses a server to process it and relays the response. The next request that that same client makes may be assigned to a completely different server. After all, that's the benefit of having a load balancer: It distributes requests among all of our machines.

Sometimes, however, we want the user to continue to be sent to the same server for the duration of their session. Maybe we've initialized and stored a session for them on the first server that they used. It may contain their logged-in status and load-balancing them to a new server would log them out. In cases like these, we want to remember which one they were sent to originally and stick them to that machine. This is called session persistence or stickiness.

In this chapter, we'll cover the following topics:

- Basing persistence on a cookie stored with the client
- Basing persistence on the client's source IP address
- Redispatching to another server when a connection can't be made
- Forcing persistence to a specific server in order to troubleshoot it
- Ignoring persistence for some types of files

Using a cookie to stick to a server

The most dependable way to remember which server a client originally connected to is to store a cookie in their browser. Then, on subsequent requests, we'll check the value of the cookie and match it against unique labels we've assigned to our servers. Whichever one matches will be the server that we always send them to. In this way, we can ensure that a client retains their session data and is not switched to a different server.

The first thing to do is add a `cookie` directive to a `backend` in order to define the properties of the cookie. Its first parameter is what to name it, which can be whatever you like, such as SERVERUSED, as shown:

```
backend webservers
  cookie SERVERUSED insert indirect nocache
```

Adding the `insert` parameter ensures that the load balancer will create the cookie, rather than relying on the backend server to do so. The `indirect` parameter tells HAProxy to remove the cookie before the message is forwarded to the server. That way the process is completely seamless and self-contained. The `nocache` parameter means that a Cache-Control: private HTTP header will be sent to the client so that the cookie won't be cached by intermediary proxies. Otherwise, all users may have gotten the same, cached cookie.

Next, we need to set the value of the cookie to something that will help identify the server that was used. This is accomplished by adding a `cookie` parameter to each `server` line followed by a unique label. In the following snippet, the first `server` stores the text web1, while the second stores web2. When the client makes another request, their cookie will be matched against these values.

```
backend webservers
  cookie SERVERUSED insert indirect nocache
  server web1 192.168.50.10:80 check cookie web1
  server web2 192.168.50.11:80 check cookie web2
```

Now the client will continue to be directed to the same server so long as their cookie exists, which is until they close their browser. Keep in mind that this type of persistence only works when using `mode http` because cookies are part of the HTTP protocol.

An alternative to having HAProxy create the cookie is to piggyback on an existing one such as a server's session cookie. Change the `cookie` directive to use the name of an existing cookie and add the `prefix` parameter. This will prepend the label we assigned to the given cookie.

```
backend webservers
  cookie JSESSIONID prefix nocache
  server web1 192.168.50.10:80 check cookie web1
  server web2 192.168.50.11:80 check cookie web2
```

In this example, we are using Java on the backend server, which happens to name its session cookies JSESSIONID. Other Web servers will use different names such as ASP.NET_SessionId for ASP.NET websites. An updated cookie would have a value that looks like this:

```
web1~BAh7CUkiD3N1c3Npb25faWQGOgZFVEkiRTg4O...
```

The web1 part will be removed before the message is forwarded to the server so that it sees the same cookie that it created. In that way, persistence is a completely seamless and invisible process from the server's perspective.

Using a stick-table for server persistence

Storing a cookie is a guaranteed way to persist a client to the first server that they're sent to. Even users behind a shared proxy or router, who share an IP address, will get unique cookies. This ensures that we can maintain a session to a single machine, while also distributing traffic equally among all of our servers. Sometimes, though, we can't use this feature. This certainly applies when we're using `mode tcp` because cookies are an HTTP phenomenon.

If we can't use cookies, we can use a `stick-table` instead. A `stick-table` is a database within HAProxy that stores some information about the client. Typically, we'll store their IP address. It's not guaranteed to be distinct because multiple clients may be behind a router that's NATing their addresses. Therefore, all clients that share an IP may be sent to the same server. For our purposes, that's okay. We don't require precision. However, this may lead to one server receiving more requests than the others.

CHAPTER 7. SERVER PERSISTENCE

In the following example, we use a `stick-table` directive to store each client's IP address and match it with a server.

```
backend webservers
  mode tcp
  server web1 192.168.50.10:80 check
  server web2 192.168.50.11:80 check
  stick-table type ip size 1m expire 30m
  stick match src
  stick store-request src
```

The `stick-table` directive specifies a `type` that defines the data that will be stored in it. Possible values are summarized in the table below:

Type	Meaning
ip	Stores IPv4 addresses
ipv6	Stores IPv6 addresses
integer	Stores 32-bit integers
string	Stores strings up to 32 characters, although a `len` parameter can be added to change the length
binary	Stores binary blocks up to 32 bytes, although a `len` parameter can be added to change the length

In the previous example, we declared a `stick-table` with `type` ip so that we can store the client's IPv4 address. The `size` parameter sets how many bytes of IP addresses we'd like to store before letting HAProxy clear out the oldest. Here, I've set it to one megabyte. We can use kilobytes (`k`), megabytes (`m`), or gigabytes (`g`). Each entry requires about 50 bytes of memory. The `expire` attribute also helps us keep memory low by clearing out any entries that haven't been matched within the specified amount of time, in this case 30 minutes. You can also set this in seconds (`s`), hours (`h`) or days (`d`).

To add data to the table, use a `stick store-request` directive, combining it with the `src` fetch method to get the client's source IP address.

```
stick store-request src
```

An entry will be added that stores the user's IP address and the server that they were sent to. To recall that information on subsequent requests, add the `stick match` directive. This queries the table using the incoming IP address to get the server that we should send them to.

```
stick match src
```

It is important that `stick match` comes before `stick store-request` in your configuration because the rules are checked in order from top to bottom. We want to check for a match before storing the current request or else we'll always overwrite our entry with the last-used server.

We can also use the more concise `stick on` directive, which combines the attributes of a `stick store-request` and `stick match`. In the following example, we use a `stick on` directive with the `src` fetch method to both store and match on the client's IP.

```
backend webservers
  mode tcp
  server web1 192.168.50.10:80 check
  server web2 192.168.50.11:80 check
  stick-table type ip size 1m expire 30m
  stick on src
```

A `stick-table` can be shared across `backend` sections. We could utilize this to define a `backend` for the sole purpose of storing our persistence records. The `stick store-request`, `stick match` and `stick on` directives have a `table` parameter that's used to reference a `stick-table` from another `backend`. In the next snippet, we keep our `stick-table` in a `backend` section called mystorage and then reference it in our webservers `backend`.

```
backend mystorage
  stick-table type ip size 1m expire 30m

backend webservers
  server web1 192.168.50.10:80 check
  server web2 192.168.50.11:80 check
  stick match src table mystorage
  stick store-request src table mystorage
```

Redispatching to another server

When we use a `stick-table` or a `cookie`, the client will stick to the first `server` that they're sent to. However, when that server fails we need a way to send them somewhere else. If we've enabled health monitoring with the `server` directive's `check` parameter, then the client will be rerouted as soon as we've detected that the server is down, regardless of whether they've established a persistent connection or not. That's because if their cookie doesn't match an available server, it is overwritten. Similarly, if their entry in the `stick-table` doesn't match an available server, it is overwritten. However, that might take several seconds depending on the interval and threshold of our health checks.

The `option redispatch` directive does not wait for the `server` to fail its health checks and be marked as down before sending the client to a working server. When added, if a client can't connect, we immediately send them to another machine. In the following snippet, we're using a `stick-table` to stick clients to the first server that they visit. In addition because we've included `option redispatch`, they will be sent to a working server as soon as their request fails to establish a connection.

```
backend webservers
   server web1 192.168.50.10:80 check
   server web2 192.168.50.11:80 check
   stick-table type ip size 1m expire 30m
   stick on src
   option redispatch
```

The nice thing about this is that if the server that failed comes back to life, we will not send them back to it, potentially causing more disruption. Instead, the client will stay with the new server for the rest of their session. The `option redispatch` directive works with both `stick-table` and `cookie` persistence.

How long the client waits before being rerouted depends largely on how long it takes for the connection to time out. This is controlled with the `timeout connect` directive in the `defaults` section. In the following snippet, a client would wait for roughly five seconds before the connection timed out.

```
defaults
  timeout connect 5s
```

Note that `option redispatch` will only redirect clients when there's a failure to connect. It doesn't apply when getting failed HTTP responses such as 500 Internal Server Error. For that, we have to wait for HTTP health checks to detect that the server is responding with errors and take the server offline.

Forcing persistence on a down server

Although we'll definitely want to route traffic away from failed servers, even for clients who have established persistent sessions, we'll probably want to allow ourselves to reach them so that we can diagnose the problem. For that, we turn to the `use-server` and `force-persist` directives.

In the following example, we have a `use-server` directive for each `server` in the `backend`. These instruct HAProxy to disregard the normal way in which it would choose a server and to instead use the given one if the condition is true. I'm using the `url_param` fetch method to get the value of a URL parameter that I've arbitrarily named serv. If serv equals 1, we are sent to the web1 server. If it matches 2, we're routed to the web2 server. Otherwise, the normal load-balancing behavior chooses where to send us.

```
backend webservers
  mode http
  option httpchk
  option redispatch
  balance roundrobin
  cookie SERVERUSED insert indirect nocache
  server web1 192.168.50.10:80 check cookie web1
  server web2 192.168.50.11:80 check cookie web2
  use-server web1 if { url_param(serv) eq 1 }
  use-server web2 if { url_param(serv) eq 2 }
  force-persist if { url_param(offline) eq true }
```

Ordinarily, a `use-server` directive will only send traffic to the specified server if it is up. Since we want to troubleshoot the server when it is down due to a server error, or

CHAPTER 7. SERVER PERSISTENCE

intentionally disabled, we need a way to get around this. Adding the `force-persist` directive means: Send it to that server anyway, so long as the `if` statement evaluates to true. The `force-persist` directive here also uses the `url_param` fetch method, this time to get a parameter I've chosen to call offline. If it's equal to true then we'll go ahead and send the request to the down server.

Now when we request the URL http://mywebsite.com/?serv=2&offline=true, we'll be sent to web2 even if it's down or disabled. We have some leeway here. Instead of using `url_param` in our `force-persist`, we could check for a cookie with the `req.cook` fetch method, check for a specific HTTP request header with `req.hdr`, or check whether the client's source IP address is within a certain range. Following are some examples of forcing persistence using these different techniques:

```
force-persist if { req.cook(offline) eq true }
force-persist if { req.hdr(X-Offline) eq true }
force-persist if { src 10.0.0.1/24 }
```

In Google Chrome, you can easily set cookies with the EditThisCookie Chrome extension and you can set HTTP request headers with the ModHeader extension.

Ignoring persistence for some files

When we make a request to a Web server for a webpage like http://mywebsite.com/, there's typically code that runs on the server to handle processing that URL, converting the response into HTML and sending it back to the client. Along the way, the code may retrieve and use the session data that's associated with the current user. After the HTML page is sent to the client, any links contained in that document such as references to images, JavaScript and CSS files are then sent as additional requests to be fetched from the server. Although we needed to send the client to the same server where their session was stored for the original request, these other static files can typically be handled by any of our servers. In other words, we don't really care which machine serves them.

We can set up a list of file extensions: .css, .js, .html, .png, .jpeg and so forth to exclude from server persistence so that if the client is requesting one of those types of files, we'll forward them to whichever server is available. Use the `ignore-persist` directive to exclude certain files from persistence, as in the following example:

```
backend webservers
  balance roundrobin
  cookie SERVERUSED insert indirect nocache
  server web1 192.168.50.10:80 check cookie web1
  server web2 192.168.50.11:80 check cookie web2
  ignore-persist if { path_end .css .js .html .png .jpeg }
```

The `ignore-persist` directive uses an `if` parameter to only ignore persistence if the given ACL is true. The `path_end` fetch method checks whether the URL ends with one of the given strings.

Summary

In this chapter, we learned how to stick a client to a specific server. This allows them to remain where their session or cached data is, if it's stored in memory on that machine. When using `mode http`, we can set a cookie in the client's browser in order to remember which server they visited. Otherwise, we can use a `stick-table` to store their IP address. This latter method isn't quite as precise, but is typically good enough for maintaining persistence.

We can take special measures to send a user to a working server if theirs becomes unavailable by using the `option redispatch` directive. We can also force persistence when we want to intentionally be routed to a failed server for troubleshooting purposes by combining `use-server` and `force-persist` directives. We also saw that for static files, we can ignore persistence altogether and use our load-balancing algorithm normally by using the `ignore-persist` directive.

Chapter 8

Logging

When things go wrong in your infrastructure, invariably someone will point at the load balancer. It's important to be able to get timely information about what's happening in HAProxy. The good news is that it was made with logging in mind, having built-in support for syslog. We can send our logs to the well-known syslog service and get detailed information about TCP connections and HTTP requests.

In this chapter, we'll cover the following topics:

- Sending HAProxy logs to syslog
- Shipping logs to a remote syslog server
- Splitting up logs by tag
- Getting detailed logs for TCP-based services
- Getting detailed logs for HTTP-based services
- Capturing HTTP headers and cookies in the logs
- Saving errors to another file

Sending logs to syslog

Linux distributions often come with a program called syslog that can log events to a file of your choosing or, even better, ship them off to some remote server called a syslog server where all captured data can be centralized. That way, you don't have to SSH into each of your servers to inspect the log files. Syslog also integrates with tools like Logstash and Fluentd, which can ship your logs to Elasticsearch, Graylog or other log management tools. For now, let's start off with seeing how to use syslog by itself to collect HAProxy's logged events and store them in a file.

Note that if HAProxy was installed using your system's package manager, such as apt or yum, most of what we'll cover here is already set up for you. We'll discuss everything as if we were configuring it ourselves for the first time so that we can get a better understanding of how the pieces fit together.

HAProxy comes ready to use syslog. The HAProxy executable calls syslog functions, which are written into its source code, whenever it encounters something noteworthy. These function calls create the log messages. In our /etc/haproxy/haproxy.cfg file, we need to specify where to send this data. By default, Ubuntu has a socket listening at /dev/log that we can send syslog events to. Update the /etc/haproxy/haproxy.cfg file's `global` section so that it contains a `log` directive that points to this socket.

```
global
  log /dev/log local0 info
```

The first parameter tells HAProxy where syslog is listening. For the second parameter, we pass `local0` as the facility, which identifies the program doing the logging. There are a number of predefined facilities, such as cron, mail and kern, but since there isn't a built-in facility for haproxy, we use one of the generic, any-purpose local designations. We can use the local0 through local7 facilities.

The third parameter sets the events, by level of importance, that we'd like to log. The levels, from most to least important, are: `emerg`, `alert`, `crit`, `err`, `warning`, `notice`, `info` and `debug`. We'll get the messages at and above the level we choose. For example, if we choose info, we'll capture log messages for all of the levels from info to emerg. If we omit this parameter, all messages will be logged. Remember to restart the HAProxy service via `sudo service haproxy restart` for any changes to take effect.

The next step is to get those events back from syslog and write them to a local file. Think of the syslog socket as a buffer for our messages. It will hold them until we ship them somewhere else. We'll use another program called rsyslog to watch that socket for any messages coming from HAProxy and then write them to a local file. The main rsyslog configuration file is located at /etc/rsyslog.conf. However, within

CHAPTER 8. LOGGING

that file, the following line appends any other .conf files that are in the /etc/rsyslog.d directory:

```
$IncludeConfig /etc/rsyslog.d/*.conf
```

This means that if we add a file ending in .conf within the /etc/rsyslog.d directory, it will be processed by rsyslog when it starts up. If you installed HAProxy through Ubuntu's package manager, then a file called /etc/rsyslog.d/49-haproxy.conf should already exist. If not, create it. It should contain the following:

```
# Create an additional socket in haproxy's chroot in order to allow
# logging via /dev/log to chroot'ed HAProxy processes
$AddUnixListenSocket /var/lib/haproxy/dev/log

# Send HAProxy messages to a dedicated logfile
if $programname startswith 'haproxy' then /var/log/haproxy.log
&~
```

This file instructs rsyslog to listen to the /dev/log socket for any messages that come from HAProxy and write them to a file called /var/log/haproxy.log. If that file doesn't already exist, it will be created automatically. Notice that we're referencing the path /var/lib/haproxy/dev/log instead of /dev/log. That's because the default HAProxy configuration runs the program within a chroot, which is a way of keeping the executable confined to a certain directory. We'll cover that in more detail later on. If you decide to change the rsyslog file, be sure to restart the rsyslog service with the following command:

```
~$ sudo service rsyslog restart
```

Next, in our /etc/haproxy/haproxy.cfg file, we need to declare which `frontend` and `backend` sections we'd like to capture log information from. We can define a `log` directive with destination, facility and level in each `frontend` and `backend` section, which would override the `log` directive that we defined in the `global` section. We can also add a `log global` directive to reuse the `global` one. We'll set `log global` in the `defaults` section so that it applies across the board, like so:

```
defaults
  log global

frontend mywebsite
  bind *:80
  default_backend webservers

backend webservers
  server web1 192.168.50.31:80
```

We can also turn off logging for a particular section by adding the `no log` directive, as shown in the following snippet:

```
frontend mywebsite
  no log
  bind *:80
  default_backend webservers
```

HAProxy logs various events such as when a client makes a request. Here's an example entry that would be written to /var/log/haproxy.log:

> Aug 4 00:45:54 lb1 haproxy[3041]: Connect from 192.168.50.1:3748 to 192.168.50.30:80 (mywebsite/HTTP)

Logging to a remote syslog server

In the previous section, we saw how to send our HAProxy logs through syslog to a local file. Now, let's see how to ship that log data to a remote server so that it's stored in a convenient, central location. We could use Logstash or Fluentd to collect and ship the data, but we'll start simple and use the syslog server that's built into rsyslog.

We need a virtual machine that has HAProxy installed on it and another that we can ship our syslog events to. Let's use Vagrant to do this. The following Vagrantfile will create three Ubuntu servers: one for our load balancer, one for a Web server and a third for a syslog server.

CHAPTER 8. LOGGING

```ruby
# -*- mode: ruby -*-
# vi: set ft=ruby :

Vagrant.configure(2) do |config|
  config.vm.define "syslog1" do |syslog|
    syslog.vm.box = "boxcutter/ubuntu1604"
      syslog.vm.hostname = "syslog1"
      syslog.vm.network "private_network", ip: "192.168.50.30"
  end

  config.vm.define "web1" do |web|
    web.vm.box = "boxcutter/ubuntu1604"
      web.vm.hostname = "web1"
      web.vm.network "private_network", ip: "192.168.50.31"
  end

  config.vm.define "lb1" do |lb|
    lb.vm.box = "boxcutter/ubuntu1604"
      lb.vm.hostname = "lb1"
    lb.vm.network "private_network", ip: "192.168.50.32"
  end
end
```

Call `vagrant up` within the directory where you created the Vagrantfile to create the three virtual machines. After they're initialized, we'll be able to SSH into each one to set them up. Next, let's set up our remote syslog server. SSH into the syslog1 server with the `vagrant ssh` command and edit the /etc/rsyslog.conf file. We will configure rsyslog to listen for incoming log messages. Uncomment the following `module` and `input` lines in order to load the imudp module and begin listening on UDP port 514.

```
# provides UDP syslog reception
module(load="imudp")
input(type="imudp" port="514")
```

Then create a new file called haproxy.conf to the /etc/rsyslog.d directory. Add the following line to it so that HAProxy messages will be logged to the file /var/log/haproxy.log:

CHAPTER 8. LOGGING

```
if $programname startswith 'haproxy' then /var/log/haproxy.log
```

Restart rsyslog with the following command:

```
~$ sudo service rsyslog restart
```

Next, SSH into the web1 virtual machine and install the NGINX Web server with the following commands:

```
~$ sudo apt update
~$ sudo apt install nginx -y
```

Now SSH into the lb1 virtual machine and install HAProxy. Then edit the configuration file /etc/haproxy/haproxy.cfg so that it contains the following settings:

```
global
  log 192.168.50.30:514 local0 info

defaults
  log global
  mode http
  timeout connect 5s
  timeout client 120s
  timeout server 120s

frontend mywebsite
  bind *:80
  default_backend webservers

backend webservers
  balance roundrobin
  server web1 192.168.50.31:80
```

Restart HAProxy:

```
~$ sudo service haproxy restart
```

CHAPTER 8. LOGGING   107

Our `backend` server points to the 192.168.50.31 IP address where we set up NGINX. Notice that the `log` directive in the `global` section specifies the IP address and UDP port where our syslog server is listening. We can omit the port and it will default to 514.

SSH into the syslog virtual machine. If we watch the /var/log/haproxy.log file on our syslog server, such as with the command `tail -f /var/log/haproxy.log`, we should see messages from HAProxy show up when we visit 192.168.50.32 in our Web browser. Here's an example log message:

> Aug 4 22:55:00 192.168.50.30 haproxy[2004]: Connect from 192.168.50.1:5598 to 192.168.50.30:80 (mywebsite/HTTP)

Splitting up log messages by tag

When rsyslog receives events from HAProxy, it checks its configuration to know which log file to write them to. Consider a portion of the following rsyslog configuration:

```
# Send HAProxy messages to a dedicated logfile
if $programname startswith 'haproxy' then /var/log/haproxy.log
```

This rule says that rsyslog should write to the file /var/log/haproxy.log when the events come from a program named haproxy. Suppose, however, that we wanted to split up our logs into different files based on which of our websites was generating the event. In our HAProxy configuration file, /etc/haproxy/haproxy.cfg, we can tag each `frontend` so that its log messages show up with a different `$programname`. Use the `log-tag` directive to differentiate each section. In the following example, the first `frontend` sets a `log-tag` to shoes, while the second sets a `log-tag` to hats.

```
frontent www.shoes.com
   bind 192.168.50.31:80
   default_backend shoe_servers
   log-tag shoes

frontend www.hats.com
   bind 192.168.50.33:80
```

```
    default_backend hat_servers
    log-tag hats
```

We can now update the rsyslog configuration file to write to different files based on the `$programname` value that comes through. We'll keep the original rule for any proxies that don't specify a `log-tag` directive.

```
# Send messages to files based on their tag
if $programname startswith 'haproxy' then /var/log/haproxy.log
if $programname == 'shoes' then /var/log/haproxy_shoes.log
if $programname == 'hats' then /var/log/haproxy_hats.log
```

Restart the rsyslog service:

```
~$ sudo service rsyslog restart
```

When you make requests to the different websites, events will be written to either haproxy_shoes.log or haproxy_hats.log in the /var/log folder.

Better TCP logging

We don't get very much information in our logs when we use `mode tcp`. To see this, let's set up a proxy in front of an instance of MySQL. Create an Ubuntu virtual machine and install the MySQL database onto it using the following commands:

```
~$ sudo apt update
~$ sudo apt install mysql-server -y
```

You'll be asked to set a password for the root database user. When the installation completes, check that the service is running with the `service mysql status` command:

```
~$ sudo service mysql status
```

Next, install HAProxy and edit the /etc/haproxy/haproxy.cfg file so that it contains the following:

```
global
  log /dev/log local0 info

defaults
  log global
  timeout connect 5000
  timeout client  50000
  timeout server  50000

frontend mydatabase_admin
  mode tcp
  timeout client 5m
  bind *:33306
  default_backend mysqlservers_admin

backend mysqlservers_admin
  mode tcp
  balance leastconn
  timeout server 5m
  server db1 127.0.0.1:3306
```

This configuration sets up a `backend` that connects to the local instance of MySQL on port 3306. It sets up a reverse proxy for this database listening on port 33306.

Notice that we've added a five-minute timeout to the `frontend` and `backend` by using `timeout client` and `timeout server`. Since we're going to be connecting to the database through the MySQL Workbench management tool, we need longer idle timeouts so that the connection is kept alive between executing queries. You would not do this when load balancing short-lived connections to the database, such as those from your website or application.

Restart the HAProxy service so that these changes take effect. Next, on your host machine, download and install MySQL Workbench so that we can connect to the database. You can download it from http://dev.mysql.com/downloads/workbench.

Run MySQL Workbench, open the menu Database | Manage connections... and click the New button at the bottom. Enter a name for the connection, the IP address of your HAProxy server and 33306 for the port.

Click the Close button and then go to Database | Connect to database.... Choose the connection you just created and click OK. When we first connect to the database,

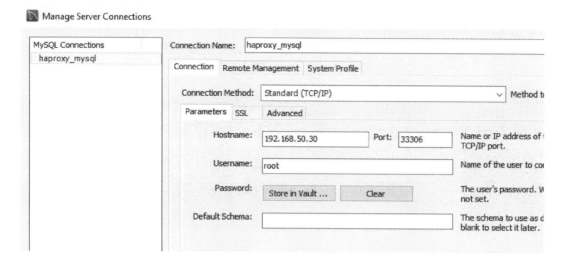

Figure 8.1: MySQL Workbench

we see new entries in the /var/log/haproxy.log file:

Aug 6 13:02:25 192.168.50.30 haproxy[2659]: Connect from 192.168.50.1:13507 to 192.168.50.30:33306 (mydatabase/TCP)

Querying the database does not add anything new because in `mode tcp`, we can only see connections in the log. However, we can get better information about those connections. Add `option tcplog` to the `defaults` section in your HAProxy configuration file.

```
defaults
  log global
  timeout connect 5000
  timeout client  50000
  timeout server  50000
  option tcplog
```

Now, our log will show entries like the following:

Aug 6 13:05:35 192.168.50.30 haproxy[2678]: 192.168.50.1:13522 [06/Aug/2016:13:05:31.724] mydatabase mysqlservers/db1 1/0/3410 1379 -- 1/1/1/1/0 0/0

The parts of the new log format break down as follows:

Field	Example
Process name and PID	haproxy[2678]
Client IP : port	192.168.50.1:13522
"[" Accept date "]"	[06/Aug/2016:13:05:31.724]
Frontend name	mydatabase
Backend name / server name	mysqlservers/db1
Time spent queued (-1 if aborted) (ms)	1
Time to connect to backend server (ms)	0
Total time taken from start to finish (ms)	3410
Bytes read	1379
Session state when ended	--
Total concurrent connections	1
Concurrent connections on frontend	1
Concurrent connections on backend	1
Active connections on server	1
Connection retries	0
Queued requests for this server	0
Queued requests for this backend	0

This gives you a better idea about how many connections were queued and being processed when you connected. It also shows how long the connection lasted and which backend server was used. All of this can be helpful when debugging issues with your TCP-based services like MySQL.

Better HTTP logging

We've seen how our logs can be fairly sparse when using `mode tcp`. The same holds true when using `mode http`. The logs don't give us much. They only show us that a connection was made between the client and the server.

Set up two virtual machines with one bound to IP address 192.168.50.30 and the other to 192.168.50.31. Install NGINX on the machine listening on the first IP and HAProxy on the one listening at the second. Then update HAProxy's configuration file, /etc/haproxy/haproxy.cfg, so that it contains the following:

CHAPTER 8. LOGGING

```
global
  log /dev/log local0 info

defaults
  log global
  timeout connect 5000
  timeout client  50000
  timeout server  50000

frontend mywebsite
  bind 192.168.50.30:80
  default_backend webservers

backend webservers
  balance roundrobin
  server web1 192.168.50.31:80 check
```

When we browse to the NGINX-hosted website at http://192.168.50.30, the following entry is added to /var/log/haproxy.log:

> Aug 8 21:26:24 lb1 haproxy[1954]: Connect from 192.168.50.1:15458 to 192.168.50.30:80 (mywebsite/HTTP)

We can enable better logging by adding the `option httplog` directive to the `defaults` section.

```
defaults
  log global
  timeout connect 5000
  timeout client  50000
  timeout server  50000
  option httplog
```

Our log will now show entries like this:

> Aug 8 21:18:06 lb1 haproxy[1930]: 192.168.50.1:15412 [08/Aug/2016:21:17:55.310] mywebsite web servers/web1 10955/0/0/0/10955 304 189 - - —- 1/1/0/1/0 0/0 "GET / HTTP/1.1"

CHAPTER 8. LOGGING

We get much more detailed information about the HTTP request and response. The parts of the previous log entry break down as follows:

Field	Example
Process name and PID	haproxy[1930]
Client IP : port	192.168.50.1:15412
"[" Accept date "]"	[08/Aug/2016:21:17:55.310]
Frontend name	mywebsite
Backend name / server name	webservers/web1
Time for client to send request (ms)	10955
Time spent queued (-1 if aborted) (ms)	0
Time to connect to backend server (ms)	0
Time for server to send response (ms)	0
Total time taken (ms)	10955
Status code	304
Bytes read	189
Captured request cookie ("-" if not captured)	-
Captured response cookie ("-" if not captured)	-
Session state when ended	——
Total concurrent connections	1
Concurrent connections on frontend	1
Concurrent connections on backend	0
Active connections on server	1
Connection retries	0
Queued requests for this server	0
Queued requests for this backend	0
"{" Captured request headers "}", blank if not captured	
"{" Captured response headers "}", blank if not captured	
HTTP method, path and version	GET / HTTP/1.1

You have the option of adding `clf` to the end of the `option httplog` directive to format the messages using the Common Log Format. Some log parsers have an easier time parsing that style. Update your configuration to have the following line in the `defaults` section.

```
option httplog clf
```

CHAPTER 8. LOGGING

Be sure to restart the HAProxy service using `sudo service haproxy restart`. Here is how events will be logged now:

> Aug 8 21:47:23 lb1 haproxy[1978]: 192.168.50.1 - - [09/Aug/2016:01:47:23 +0000] "GET / HTTP/1.1" 304 189 "" "" 15615 301 "mywebsite" "webservers" "web1" 5 0 4 14 23 —— 1 1 0 1 0 0 0 "" ""

This new format is as follows:

Field	Example
Process name and PID	haproxy[1978]
Client IP	192.168.50.1
Always a dash	-
Always a dash	-
"[" Accept date "]"	[09/Aug/2016:01:47:23 +0000]
HTTP method, path and version	GET / HTTP/1.1
Status code	304
Bytes read	189
Always an empty string	""
Always an empty string	""
Client port	15615
Milliseconds part of accept date	301
Frontend name	"mywebsite"
Backend name	"webservers"
server name	"web1"
Time for client to send request (ms)	5
Time spent queued (-1 if aborted) (ms)	0
Time to connect to backend server (ms)	4
Time for server to send response (ms)	14
Total time taken (ms)	23
Session state when ended	——
Total concurrent connections	1
Concurrent connections on frontend	1
Concurrent connections on backend	0
Active connections on server	1
Connection retries	0
Queued requests for this server	0
Queued requests for this backend	0

Field	Example
Captured request cookie	""
Captured response cookie	""

Note that we can capture cookies and HTTP headers to display in the log, but in this example, we didn't have any to show. In the next section, we will show how to specify the cookies and headers that we want to see in the log.

Logging cookies and headers

In this section, we'll see how to log the values that were set for HTTP headers and cookies as they passed through the load balancer. Note that for this to work, you must also set the `option httplog` directive. Let's add a `capture cookie` directive to our `frontend` to capture a cookie's value in the log. This directive can only go into a `frontend` or `listen` section and is not allowed in the `defaults`.

In the following example, we're using `capture cookie` to log the value of a cookie called SERVERUSED. This happens to be our server persistence cookie that's defined in our webservers `backend`.

```
frontend mywebsite
  bind 192.168.50.30:80
  default_backend webservers
  capture cookie SERVERUSED len 32

backend webservers
  balance roundrobin
  cookie SERVERUSED insert indirect nocache
  server web1 192.168.50.31:80 check cookie web1
```

The format is `capture cookie <name> len <length>` where name is the name of the cookie and length is the maximum number of characters to capture of the cookie's value. Beware that we can only capture one cookie at a time per `frontend`. In our /var/log/haproxy.log file, we should now see the value of our SERVERUSED cookie:

> Aug 8 23:33:32 lb1 haproxy[2300]: 192.168.50.1:16600 [08/Aug/2016:23:33:30.872] mywebsite webservers/web1 1956/0/0/3/1959 304 220 **SERVERUSED=web1** - –VN 1/1/0/1/0 0/0 "GET / HTTP/1.1"

We can log HTTP headers by using the `capture request header` and `capture response header` directives. The format is: `capture request header <name> len <length>`. Unlike cookies, we can log any number of headers. They'll show up in the log between curly braces. The names of the headers won't be saved, but they'll be in the same order as they appear in the configuration. In the following snippet, we log the Host and User-Agent request headers and the X-Powered-By response header.

```
frontend mywebsite
  bind 192.168.50.30:80
  default_backend webservers
  capture request header Host len 32
  capture request header User-Agent len 32
  capture response header X-Powered-By len 32
```

The log might look like this:

> Aug 8 23:48:30 lb1 haproxy[2324]: 192.168.50.1:16687 [08/Aug/2016:23:48:30.238] mywebsite webservers/web1 2/0/0/1/3 304 209 - - –NI 1/1/0/1/0 0/0 **{192.168.50.30|Mozilla/5.0 (Windows NT 10.0; WOW64) AppleWebKit/537.36 (KHTML, } {web1}** "GET / HTTP/1.1"

Notice that the two request header values are listed together, separated by a pipe character: `{192.168.50.30|Mozilla/5.0 (Windows NT 10.0; WOW64) AppleWebKit/537.36 (KHTML, }`. Also note that the User-Agent is cut off at 32 characters since that's what we set the limit to. The X-Powered-By response header, which has a value of web1, is in its own set of curly braces.

Separating errors into their own log file

When capturing log information from HAProxy, one problem is the sheer amount of the data that we'll receive. To help, we can separate the more relevant information,

CHAPTER 8. LOGGING

which typically includes timeouts, retries and failed HTTP requests into a separate log file. The trick is marking it in a way so that it's easy to distinguish from the informational, less critical information that fills up our logs. For that, we can elevate all noteworthy events to the syslog status of err. Then, we'll have rsyslog write them to a dedicated file.

Add an `option log-separate-errors` directive to the `defaults` section in your /etc/haproxy/haproxy.cfg file so that all interesting events are categorized as err.

```
global
  log /dev/log local0 info

defaults
  log global
  option log-separate-errors
```

Recall that there are eight syslog severity levels. From most important to least, they are: `emerg`, `alert`, `crit`, `err`, `warning`, `notice`, `info` and `debug`. Ordinarily, if our Web server returned an HTTP 500 Internal Server Error response, it would only show up in our load balancer's logs if we were capturing info level events and above. However, with the `option log-separate-errors` directive, they'll be categorized as err instead.

If you installed HAProxy through your system's package manager, then you should already have an rsyslog configuration file for it at /etc/rsyslog.d/49-haproxy.conf. This file contains the following:

```
# Send HAProxy messages to a dedicated logfile
if $programname startswith 'haproxy' then /var/log/haproxy.log
```

To have rsyslog store errors in a different file, we can filter by syslog severity level. Each level has a corresponding number, as described in the following table:

number	severity level
0	Emergency
1	Alert
2	Critical
3	Error

number	severity level
4	Warning
5	Notice
6	Informational
7	Debug

Let's add another line to the 49-haproxy.conf file so that it checks for any events that have a level of three or higher. We can use a variable called `$syslogseverity` to get this number. For space, I've split it onto two lines, but it should go onto one.

```
# Send HAProxy messages to a dedicated logfile
if $programname startswith 'haproxy' then /var/log/haproxy.log

if $programname startswith 'haproxy' and $syslogseverity <= 3
  then /var/log/haproxy_errors.log
```

Now the /var/log/haproxy.log file will receive all messages including errors, but errors will also be recorded in /var/log/haproxy_errors.log. You can find information about other rsyslog properties at http://www.rsyslog.com/doc/v8-stable/configuration/properties.html.

Summary

In this chapter, we learned how to configure HAProxy to log events using syslog. This allows messages to be buffered and then written to log files without slowing down incoming requests. We can extend this so that our logs are shipped to a remote syslog server, which allows us to aggregate log data in a central location.

We then learned that, by default, we only log basic information about our TCP and HTTP-based services. However, we can turn on more detailed logging by adding the `option tcplog` and `option httplog` directives. We can also capture the values of HTTP headers and cookies with the `capture cookie`, `capture request header` and `capture response header` directives.

Last, we saw how to separate interesting events, such as failed HTTP requests, into their own log file by using the `option log-separate-errors` directive. The ability for HAProxy to integrate with syslog makes for a flexible and powerful method of capturing events.

Chapter 9

SSL and TLS

As you are probably aware, Secure Sockets Layer (SSL) and Transport Layer Security (TLS) are protocols that allow for securing traffic as it travels over a network or the Internet. They ensure that communication is kept secret and is protected from being tampered with it. They also ensure that you are connecting to the website or service that you think you are. If not, you'll typically get a warning message telling you that the communication cannot be trusted.

TLS is newer and more secure than SSL. These days, you should only use TLS even though we often still use the term SSL to describe it. From here on out, I will try to stick to using the term TLS unless specifically talking about the obsolete protocol SSL.

In this chapter, we will cover the following topics:

- Using TLS passthrough so that the backend servers handle all aspects of encryption and decryption

- Enabling TLS termination, wherein traffic is encrypted and decrypted at the load balancer

- Encrypting and decrypting at the load balancer, but then re-encrypting messages before sending them to the backend servers

- Redirecting from insecure HTTP to secure HTTPS

- Restricting the versions of SSL and TLS that can be used

- Restricting the SSL and TLS ciphers that can be used

TLS passthrough

In this section, we'll talk about setting up TLS passthrough, wherein the backend servers are responsible for all aspects of encrypting and decrypting communication between themselves and the client. HAProxy, which sits in the middle, simply passes the messages through as a Layer 4 proxy. It will not be able to inspect the content of the requests or responses. You'd use this with services that don't communicate over HTTP and with which you'd have to use `mode tcp` anyway. For example, the MySQL database communicates over TCP, but can use TLS to encrypt the queries as they travel over a network.

As far as configuration goes, there's not much that needs to be done to enable SSL passthrough. When we use `mode tcp`, it doesn't matter to HAProxy whether the traffic is encrypted or not. As a Layer 4 reverse proxy, all it needs to worry about is connecting the client to the correct backend server. The messages that pass over that connection are none of its concern.

Let's set up a MySQL database that uses TLS. Then we'll have HAProxy relay that communication without needing to decrypt it. We can use the following Vagrantfile to set up two machines: one for HAProxy and the other for MySQL:

```ruby
# -*- mode: ruby -*-
# vi: set ft=ruby :

Vagrant.configure("2") do |config|

  config.vm.define "haproxy" do |machine|
    machine.vm.box = "boxcutter/ubuntu1604"
    machine.vm.network "private_network", ip: "192.168.50.11"
  end

  config.vm.define "database" do |machine|
    machine.vm.box = "boxcutter/ubuntu1604"
    machine.vm.network "private_network", ip: "192.168.50.12"
  end
end
```

Call `vagrant up` to create the two virtual machines and then SSH into the database machine by using the `vagrant ssh` command:

CHAPTER 9. SSL AND TLS

```
~$ vagrant up
~$ vagrant ssh database
```

Once logged into the database VM, install MySQL by using the apt package manager:

```
~$ sudo apt update
~$ sudo apt install mysql-server -y
```

We need to generate an X.509 certificate and private key before MySQL can use TLS. The certificate is used to encrypt the communication. The private key, which only the server has access to, decrypts it. Together, these are known as a key-pair. To get one, you've got several options: You can buy a TLS key-pair from a number of vendors after generating a certificate signing request (CSR), get a free one from https://letsencrypt.org, or have MySQL generate a self-signed certificate and key. The last option works well for test environments like ours.

We'll use the `mysql_ssl_rsa_setup` command that ships with MySQL to generate a new self-signed certificate and private key.

```
~$ sudo mkdir /etc/mysql/ssl
~$ sudo mysql_ssl_rsa_setup --datadir=/etc/mysql/ssl --uid=mysql
```

The files will be saved in the directory we specify with the `--datadir` parameter. Be sure to create that directory first. The `--uid` parameter sets the owner of the generated files to mysql, which is the user account that MySQL runs as. You should now have a number of PEM files in the /etc/mysql/ssl directory. Next, we need to tell MySQL to look here when configuring TLS. Add the following lines to the /etc/mysql/mysql.conf.d/mysqld.cnf file in order to tell MySQL where to find our PEM files.

```
ssl-ca=/etc/mysql/ssl/ca.pem
ssl-cert=/etc/mysql/ssl/server-cert.pem
ssl-key=/etc/mysql/ssl/server-key.pem
```

Also, update the file so that the `bind-address` line is commented out. Comments are designated by adding a pound sign to the beginning of the line, like so:

CHAPTER 9. SSL AND TLS

```
# bind-address = 127.0.0.1
```

The `bind-address` line restricts the IP address we can use to connect to MySQL. Since we want to connect over the IP 192.168.50.12, and not just 127.0.0.1, we must comment out this line so that MySQL is accessible over all IP addresses. Restart the MySQL service so that these changes take effect.

```
~$ sudo service mysql restart
```

We must log into MySQL and create a user account that is allowed to access the database remotely. Use the following command to log in. It will prompt you to enter the password that you set when installing MySQL.

```
~$ mysql -uroot -p
```

Once logged in, use the following command to create a new user named remoteuser that has access to query the database from a remote machine. Notice that we are setting the `REQUIRE SSL` option so that this user must connect using SSL/TLS.

```
mysql> GRANT ALL PRIVILEGES ON *.* TO 'remoteuser'@'%'
   IDENTIFIED BY 'mypassword' REQUIRE SSL;
```

To verify that TLS is enabled, we can query the database using the `SHOW VARIABLES` command, like so:

```
mysql> SHOW VARIABLES LIKE '%ssl%';
```

It should return a list of variables including `have_openssl` and `have_ssl`, which should be set to YES.

```
+---------------+-----------------------------+
| Variable_name | Value                       |
+---------------+-----------------------------+
| have_openssl  | YES                         |
| have_ssl      | YES                         |
| ssl_ca        | /etc/mysql/ssl/ca.pem       |
```

CHAPTER 9. SSL AND TLS

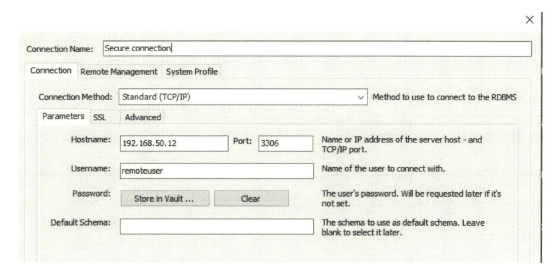

Figure 9.1: MySQL Workbench connection

```
| ssl_capath    |                              |
| ssl_cert      | /etc/mysql/ssl/server-cert.pem |
| ssl_cipher    |                              |
| ssl_crl       |                              |
| ssl_crlpath   |                              |
| ssl_key       | /etc/mysql/ssl/server-key.pem |
+---------------+------------------------------+
9 rows in set (0.00 sec)
```

Let's try connecting to this database. On your host machine, install MySQL Workbench. You can download it from http://dev.mysql.com/downloads/workbench. Run MySQL Workbench and open the menu Database | Manage connections... and click the New button at the bottom. Enter a name for the connection, the IP address of your HAProxy server, which should be 192.168.50.12, and 3306 for the port. Set the username field to remoteuser and, if you like, store the password by clicking the Store in Vault... button.

When you click the Test Connection button, you should see SSL: enabled.

Any queries that we send to the database will now be encrypted. Let's install HAProxy on our other virtual machine and set it up to use TLS passthrough. Log into the haproxy machine with **vagrant ssh** and then use the following commands

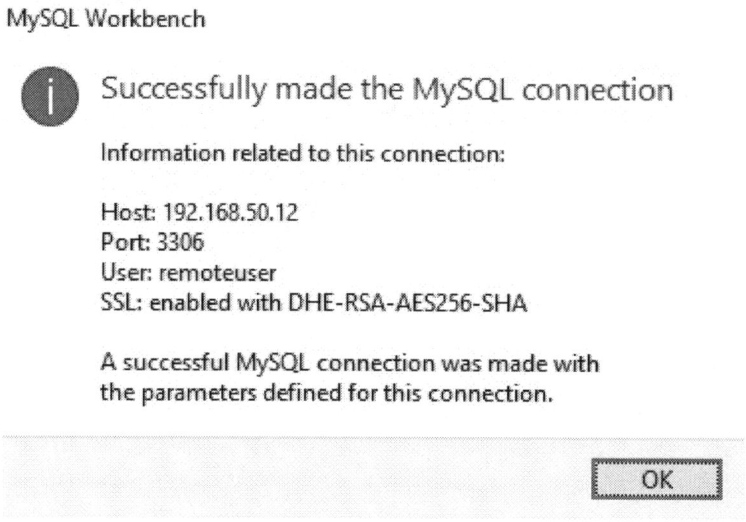

Figure 9.2: SSL enabled

to install HAProxy:

```
~$ sudo apt update
~$ sudo apt install haproxy -y
```

Update the HAProxy configuration file, /etc/haproxy/haproxy.cfg, so that it contains the following:

```
frontend mydatabase
  mode tcp
  timeout client 5m
  bind *:3306
  default_backend databases

backend databases
  mode tcp
  timeout server 5m
  balance leastconn
  server db1 192.168.50.12:3306 check
```

CHAPTER 9. SSL AND TLS

The `frontend` binds to port 3306, which is the same port used by MySQL on the other VM. We use `mode tcp` for both the `frontend` and `backend`. Notice that we do not do anything special to implement TLS passthrough. It's enough to pass the traffic to the backend servers and let them handle the encryption and decryption. That's all there is to TLS passthrough.

Establishing a TLS connection can be CPU intensive and it's best to reuse it once you've got it. For that reason, consider using session persistence to prevent the client from being load balanced to another backend server, forcing them to renegotiate the TLS certificate. In the following example, we've updated the `backend` section to use a stick-table to stick the client to the first server that they visit.

```
backend databases
  mode tcp
  timeout server 5m
  balance leastconn
  stick-table type ip size 1m expire 5m
  stick on src
  server db1 192.168.50.12:3306 check
```

The client's IP address will be stored in the stick-table so that we can recall which server they visited. Upon subsequent requests, they will be directed to the same machine, until their record in the stick-table expires. In this case, the record will last for five minutes.

TLS termination

When it comes to securing Web traffic using the HTTPS protocol, HAProxy can handle all of the details of TLS encryption, rather than having your backend Web servers do it. The benefits of this include:

- easier maintenance and better security by being able to store TLS key-pairs in only one place
- lessening the work that backend servers have to do
- taking advantage of features like restricting which versions of SSL/TLS can be used

CHAPTER 9. SSL AND TLS

When HAProxy handles the encryption and decryption, traffic is free to flow to your backend servers decrypted, in the clear. Your Web servers will only need to listen for HTTP traffic and not HTTPS traffic. HAProxy will have terminated, or removed the decryption from, the TLS on its end. This simplifies your network topology overall because now your servers don't have to worry about accepting both HTTP, which typically arrives over port 80, and HTTPS, which typically arrives over port 443.

In the following example, we have a `frontend` section called mywebsite that has a `bind` directive listening on port 443 while the `backend` called webservers has `server` directives that connect over port 80. In this setup, only the `frontend` needs to worry about accepting encrypted, TLS-enabled communication.

```
frontend mywebsite
  mode http
  bind *:443 ssl crt /etc/ssl/certs/mywebsite_cert.pem
  default_backend webservers

backend webservers
  mode http
  balance roundrobin
  server web1 192.168.50.12:80 check
  server web2 192.168.50.13:80 check
```

TLS is terminated at the `frontend` by including the `ssl` parameter on the `bind` directive. The `crt` parameter designates the PEM file to use, which should be a file containing the TLS public certificate and private key. All of the usual rules apply to the certificate you use: It must have a Common Name that matches your Web site's domain name. It must be signed by a trusted certificate authority, although self-signing works for testing. On Linux, use the following command to create a self-signed certificate by using OpenSSL:

```
~$ openssl req -x509 -sha256 -nodes -days 365 -newkey rsa:2048
    -keyout mywebsite_key.pem -out mywebsite_cert.pem
```

When you execute this command, you'll be asked a series of questions that will be put into your certificate. The one that asks for a Common Name should be set to your website's domain name, such as mywebsite.com.

```
Generating a 2048 bit RSA private key
.............................................+++
.....................................................+++
writing new private key to 'mywebsite_key.pem'
-----
You are about to be asked to enter information that will be incorporated
into your certificate request.
What you are about to enter is what is called a Distinguished Name or a DN.
There are quite a few fields but you can leave some blank
For some fields there will be a default value,
If you enter '.', the field will be left blank.
-----
Country Name (2 letter code) [AU]:US
State or Province Name (full name) [Some-State]:OH
Locality Name (eg, city) []:Columbus
Organization Name (eg, company) [Internet Widgits Pty Ltd]:MyWebsite
Organizational Unit Name (eg, section) []:
Common Name (e.g. server FQDN or YOUR name) []:mywebsite.com
Email Address []:admin@test.com
```

This will create two files: mywebsite_key.pem and mywebsite_cert.pem. We must combine these files before using them with HAProxy, which we can do by reading one file with the `cat` command and appending the output to the other. It doesn't matter whether the private key or certificate comes first in the combined file.

```
~$ cat mywebsite_key.pem >> mywebsite_cert.pem
```

The result should look like this (truncated for space):

```
-----BEGIN CERTIFICATE-----
MIIDrzCCApegAwIBAgIJAPwxuTUU+qouMA0GCSqGSIb3DQEBCwUAMG4xCzAJBgNV
BAYTAlVTMQswCQYDVQQIDAJPSDERMA8GA1UEBwwIQ29sdW1idXMxDTALBgNVBAoM
BFRlc3QxETAPBgNVBAMMCHRlc3QuY29tMR0wGwYJKoZIhvcNAQkBFg5hZG1pcb...
-----END CERTIFICATE-----
-----BEGIN PRIVATE KEY-----
MIIEvAIBADANBgkqhkiG9w0BAQEFAASCBKYwggSiAgEAAoIBAQDFjY8bjC12ihBu
KNbscG8muEorcB/nQIOA9/U8rmHRMwq+KKNrfjZdvafEmc4JJ/gDnwEoLk9DNeai
fH9CfOJk5HGSlfzJl12umpgkuUDmu7RZrgofa0J4Mc1amfieGlnygERw9euw1...
-----END PRIVATE KEY-----
```

CHAPTER 9. SSL AND TLS

Copy this file to a directory where HAProxy can access it, such as to the /etc/ssl/certs directory. If you are running HAProxy in a chroot, be sure to mount this directory within your chroot'ed directory. For example, if you are running HAProxy in a chroot at /var/lib/haproxy, you would execute the following commands to mount the /etc/ssl/certs directory there:

```
~$ cd /var/lib/haproxy
~$ sudo mkdir certs
~$ sudo mount --bind /certs /etc/ssl/certs
```

On Windows, we can use the `makecert` program to create a self-signed certificate that contains the certificate and private key. Information can be found at https://msdn.microsoft.com/en-us/library/ff699202.aspx. The only problem is that this creates the file using the PFX format. However, we can copy the PFX file to a Linux machine and use the following OpenSSL command to convert it to a PEM file:

```
openssl pkcs12 -in mywebsite_cert.pfx -out mywebsite_cert.pem -nodes
```

Our `frontend` can also be configured to accept both HTTP and HTTPS traffic, while sending only decrypted traffic to the backend servers. In the following example, we bind to ports 80 and 443.

```
frontend mywebsite
  bind *:80
  bind *:443 ssl crt /etc/ssl/certs/mywebsite_cert.pem
  default_backend webservers

backend webservers
  balance roundrobin
  server web1 192.168.50.12:80 check
  server web2 192.168.50.13:80 check
```

Having a single `frontend` that handles secure and non-secure traffic is a good way to simplify your configuration.

CHAPTER 9. SSL AND TLS

TLS re-encryption

Using TLS termination means that traffic will pass in the clear over your network after the messages are decrypted at the load balancer. If you're confident that no unauthorized users can access your network, then you may be okay with that. It's certainly simpler to have TLS terminated in only one place. However, if there's a chance that internal users or attackers could sniff your network traffic, then you might be better off encrypting it from end-to-end.

TLS passthrough ensures that traffic is encrypted while traveling over the wire, but it prevents HAProxy from operating as a Layer 7 proxy. That means it can't read HTTP headers, set cookies, or otherwise interact with HTTP requests and responses. TLS re-encryption gives us another option: have HAProxy decrypt the incoming requests so that it can use all of its Layer 7 capabilities and then re-encrypt it when sending it to the backend server.

In the following example, we first use the `bind` directive's `ssl` and `crt` parameters to enable TLS termination in the `frontend`. Then, in the `backend` we add an `ssl` parameter to each `server` directive in order to turn on TLS re-encryption. Notice that we are using port 443 in both sections.

```
frontend mywebsite
  mode http
  bind *:443 ssl crt /etc/ssl/certs/mywebsite_cert.pem
  default_backend webservers

backend webservers
  mode http
  balance roundrobin
  server web1 192.168.50.12:443 check ssl
  server web2 192.168.50.13:443 check ssl
```

When we add the `ssl` parameter to a `server` directive, it causes HAProxy to act as if it were a client connecting to the Web server over HTTPS. There's just one snag. By default, HAProxy will give you the following error if the certificate that the Web server uses is not trusted:

> Verify is enabled by default but no CA file specified. If you're running on a LAN where you're certain to trust the server's certificate, please set

an explicit 'verify none' statement on the 'server' line, or use 'ssl-server-verify none' in the global section to disable server-side verifications by default.

The certificate should be signed by a trusted certificate authority so that HAProxy will be able to initiate a secure connection. This is because an implicit `verify required` is added to the `server` line. If you're using a self-signed certificate on the Web server, then you can add `verify none` like so:

```
server web1 192.168.50.12:443 check ssl verify none
```

This turns off verification of the certificate. Alternatively, you can add the `ca-file` parameter to specify a path to a PEM file that contains the CA's public certificate. A self-signed certificate can act as its own CA, though. So, we could set `ca-file` to point to our self-signed certificate:

```
server web1 192.168.50.12:443 check ssl verify required
    ca-file /etc/ssl/certs/mywebsite_cert.pem
```

Or if your server's certificate was signed with an in-house CA, you can specify its path instead:

```
server web1 192.168.50.12:443 check ssl verify required
    ca-file /etc/ssl/certs/MyCA.pem
```

After adding either `verify none` or `ca-file`, HAProxy will be able to connect to the backend server using HTTPS.

Redirecting HTTP traffic to HTTPS

Oftentimes, we want to present our website over a secure connection using HTTPS, but users are accustomed to typing a URL into their address bar that does not contain the scheme. For example, although we would prefer our users to enter https://mybankwebsite.com, they're more likely to enter mybankwebsite.com. Modern browsers detect the missing scheme and fill in the blanks with a regular, non-secure http://. In order to get users to the secure version of our site, we can redirect them to the HTTPS scheme.

CHAPTER 9. SSL AND TLS

Note that redirecting to HTTPS does not safeguard clients from having their data stolen if an attacker is able to intercept their communication before they are redirected to HTTPS. For example, as blogger and hacker Moxie Marlinspike has demonstrated with his sslstrip security tool, one can launch a man-in-the-middle attack that allows an attacker to steal data while displaying what appears to be a secure site to the client. However, until browsers begin defaulting to HTTPS, redirecting clients is better than simply denying their connection.

In the following snippet, we use the `redirect scheme` directive to change any connections that came in over HTTP to use HTTPS instead.

```
frontend mywebsite
  bind *:80
  bind *:443 ssl crt /etc/ssl/certs/mywebsite_cert.pem
  redirect scheme https if !{ ssl_fc }
  default_backend webservers

backend webservers
  balance roundrobin
  server web1 192.168.50.12:80 check
  server web2 192.168.50.13:80 check
```

Notice that we are binding to ports 80 and 443 in our `frontend`. This is essential so that we can detect the user coming in on HTTP (port 80). If we only bind to port 443, then if a user tries to connect to port 80 they'll get a Connection refused error. The `redirect scheme` directive, as you can probably tell, redirects the client to a new URL that begins with the scheme we specify.

The `ssl_fc` fetch method returns true if the connection came in over HTTPS. However, the exclamation point in front of it negates the rule so that it returns true if the client connected over HTTP. In that case, we perform the redirect. Beware that `ssl_fc` only returns true if the connection was received by a `bind` statement that has the `ssl` parameter. In other words, we have to be doing TLS termination in HAProxy. It will not work when we're using TLS passthrough or terminating TLS by some other tool like Pound or Stunnel.

Restricting versions of SSL

The oldest version of SSL that HAProxy can use is SSL 3.0. That version first appeared in 1996. In 1999, TLS 1.0 replaced SSL as a more secure protocol. That was followed by TLS 1.1 in 2006 and TLS 1.2 in 2008. It's important to restrict which versions of SSL/TLS your website accepts, since older versions are susceptible to attacks.

Before an SSL/TLS connection is made, the Web browser and server must agree on which version both can use. Older browsers, for example, don't understand the newer protocols. If a browser doesn't know how to use the latest version, it will ask the server if it wouldn't mind downgrading to an older one. If the server agrees, they can begin communicating using a mutually compatible version. This gives the widest range of interoperability with browsers and other types of clients.

However, a hacker can use this friendly downgrade mechanism as a way to force the server into using a less secure protocol. This is known as a POODLE (Padding Oracle On Downgraded Legacy Encryption) attack. They might do this as part of a man-in-the-middle attack in the hope of leveraging the obsolescence of the older protocols to decrypt traffic passing by over a public network. For that reason, you may want to decline using older protocols, even if a client asks for them. The no-sslv3 can be added to a bind directive to disallow downgrading to SSL version 3.0, as shown:

```
frontend mywebsite
  bind *:443 ssl crt /etc/ssl/certs/mywebsite_cert.pem no-sslv3
  default_backend webservers
```

We can also use the no-tlsv10, no-tlsv11 and no-tlsv12 for disabling TLS version 1.0, TLS version 1.1 and TLS version 1.2, respectively. In the following example, the proxy will not accept SSL 3.0 or TLS 1.0:

```
frontend mywebsite
  bind *:443 ssl crt /etc/ssl/certs/mywebsite_cert.pem no-sslv3 no-tlsv10
  default_backend webservers
```

Be careful not to disable all versions of SSL/TLS or the client's connection will be refused when they try to access your site over HTTPS. We can also specify

CHAPTER 9. SSL AND TLS

the `force-sslv3`, `force-tlsv10`, `force-tlsv11` or `force-tlsv12` to accept only a specific version. The following example only allows clients to connect using TLS 1.2:

```
frontend mywebsite
  bind *:443 ssl crt /etc/ssl/certs/mywebsite_cert.pem force-tlsv12
  default_backend webservers
```

Enabling only the newest version of TLS means dropping support for older browsers. Internet Explorer 6, for example, only supports up to SSL version 3.0 and cannot use TLS at all. However, the most recent versions of Chrome, Firefox, Internet Explorer and Microsoft Edge have SSL version 3.0 disabled by default. There's a good overview of which versions each browser supports on Wikipedia: https://en.wikipedia.org/wiki/Template:TLS/SSL_support_history_of_web_browsers.

You can also set the `no-*` and `force-*` directives, such as `no-sslv3` and `force-tlsv12`, for all frontends by adding a `ssl-default-bind-options` directive in the `global` section. In the next snippet, we disallow clients from using SSL 3.0 and TLS 1.0 for all of our proxies.

```
global
  ssl-default-bind-options no-sslv3 no-tlsv10
```

The settings mentioned so far only work when doing SSL/TLS termination at the load balancer. When doing TLS passthrough, wherein HAProxy acts as a Layer 4 proxy and the Web server handles the encryption and decryption on its end, we have to do things a bit differently. In that case, we can use the `req.ssl_ver` fetch method to check which version of SSL the client has requested. Then, we can reject the connection for certain values by using the `tcp-request content reject` directive. In the following example, we reject any requests that want to use SSL version 3.0:

```
frontend mywebsite
  mode tcp
  bind *:443
  default_backend webservers
  tcp-request content reject if { req.ssl_ver 3 }
```

The `req.ssl_ver` method may return the following values:

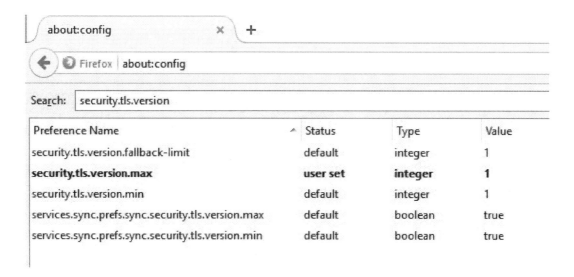

Figure 9.3: Setting Firefox's SSL/TLS version

SSL/TLS version	req.ssl_ver
SSL 3.0	3
TLS 1.0	3.1

You can reject a range of versions by separating them with a colon, as shown in the following example where we specify a `req.ssl_ver` value of 3:3.1:

```
acl wants_sslv3_or_tlsv10 req.ssl_ver 3:3.1
tcp-request content reject if wants_sslv3_or_tlsv10
```

You can test which versions of SSL/TLS your site accepts by entering its URL into the search box at https://www.ssllabs.com/ssltest. Among other things, it will tell you which browsers your configuration supports. Also, the Firefox browser allows you to change which versions it accepts, which is great for testing. Type `about:config` into your address bar, then search for the `security.tls.version` settings. Set the `security.tls.version.min` and `security.tls.version.max` to the number that corresponds to the version of SSL/TLS that you want to accept on the client side.

The Firefox values are described in the following table:

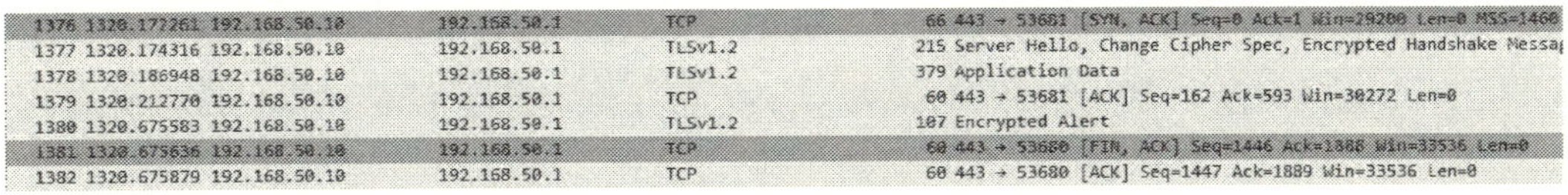

Figure 9.4: Wireshark showing TLS version

security.tls.version	What it means
0	SSL 3.0
1	TLS 1.0
2	TLS 1.1
3	TLS 1.2

As you make requests to your website, you can use Wireshark to see which version you're truly connecting with.

SSL ciphers

When TLS communication begins, a secret key is shared between the client and server so that their communication can be encrypted while traveling over the network or Internet. This is known as the TLS handshake. The cipher suite describes the process used to transfer that secret key during the handshake. It may, for example, mandate that AES256 be used to encrypt the secret key or that a block cipher be used so that encrypting the same message twice will never return the same text, which prevents hackers from building up a dictionary of known values. The rules come in many combinations, but the server and client must agree on which to use. They must both support what's being asked for and some newer cipher suites are only available in later versions of TLS. As knowledge of weaknesses in some ciphers becomes known, the preferred list of cipher suites changes.

When decrypting traffic with HAProxy, we can choose which cipher suites are acceptable by setting the `bind` directive's `ciphers` parameter. Here's an example of restricting the list of preferred cipher suites to a single one, DES-CBC3-SHA, that The Open Web Application Security Project (OWASP) says will work as a good does-the-job cipher suite:

```
frontend mywebsite
```

```
mode http
bind *:443 ssl crt /etc/haproxy/MyCert.pem ciphers DES-CBC3-SHA
default_backend webservers
```

The Internet Engineering Task Force (IETF) also has a list of cipher suites that it recommends in its RFC 2725 document. You can check it out at https://tools.ietf.org/html/rfc7525#section-4.2. However, keep in mind that these particular cipher suites are only supported when using TLS 1.2. You can set multiple ciphers by separating them with colons. Allowing multiple cipher suites lets you support more browsers.

```
ECDHE-RSA-AES256-GCM-SHA384:ECDHE-RSA-AES128-GCM-SHA256:
    DHE-RSA-AES256-GCM-SHA384:DHE-RSA-AES128-GCM-SHA256
```

Another place to see which cipher suites to use is Qualys, Inc.'s SSL Labs website, https://www.ssllabs.com/ssltest, where you can enter the name of a well-known website like amazon.com to see which cipher suites they use or your own URL to test how strong your configuration is. You'll get a grade from A to F, depending on how secure your website is. You can also get a list of available cipher suites at the OpenSSL website, https://www.openssl.org/docs/manmaster/apps/ciphers.html. Each suite is listed in both the long format, such as `TLS_RSA_WITH_3DES_EDE_CBC_SHA`, and the shorter format, such as `DES-CBC3-SHA`. Use the shorter format with HAProxy.

To set the cipher suites to use for all proxies, add the `ssl-default-bind-ciphers` directive to the `global` section, like so:

```
global
  ssl-default-bind-ciphers DES-CBC3-SHA
```

Individual `frontend` and `listen` sections can still override this default.

Summary

In this chapter, we discussed three ways to manage secure, TLS connections. The first, TLS passthrough, is ideal when using `mode tcp`, since it leaves the burden of encrypting and decrypting traffic up to the backend server. TLS termination enables

HAProxy to handle all aspect of the encryption, freeing your backend Web servers to only accept HTTP traffic. This also lets us use HAProxy as a Layer 7 proxy. If you require messages to be secured from end-to-end, you can use TLS re-encryption to encrypt between HAProxy and the client, as well as between HAProxy and the server. In this way, our load balancer is able to act as a Layer 7 proxy in the middle, while keeping traffic secure on both sides.

We saw that we can redirect clients from HTTP connections to secure HTTPS connections by using the `redirect scheme` directive. Although this doesn't completely protect our clients from eavesdropping, it does at least try to get them onto a more secure protocol. We also saw that we can limit the versions of SSL and TLS, as well as which cipher suites are used during the TLS handshake. These mechanisms ensure that we are using only the strongest measures to protect ourselves and our users.

Chapter 10

Changing the Message

When we're using the HTTP protocol, communication flows over a TCP connection. It's like a pipeline connecting the client to the server, with HAProxy sitting in the middle. This means that requests flow through the pipe in one direction and responses flow back in the other. Both pass through HAProxy on their way to their destinations. This gives us the chance to alter the HTTP request and response messages while they're in transit.

In this chapter, we will cover the following topics:

- Rewriting the URL
- Adding headers to the HTTP request
- Adding headers to the HTTP response
- Removing headers from the response
- Compressing files with gzip
- Detecting the type of device with the 51Degrees library

URL rewriting

As requests pass through HAProxy, we have the opportunity to change them in various ways before sending them on to the backend servers. In this section, we'll

CHAPTER 10. CHANGING THE MESSAGE

take a look at rewriting, or modifying, the URL. Before we get to that, it might help to refresh our memories on the structure of an HTTP request. We can use Fiddler to examine the HTTP traffic as we visit a website. You can download it at http://www.telerik.com/fiddler.

Let's suppose that you host a website at http://fineshoes.com that serves a webpage called index.html. Or, if you're running a Web server in a virtual environment, you can update your computer's /etc/hosts file, or C:/Windows/System32/drivers/etc/hosts on Windows, to map fineshoes.com to the VM's IP address. Now if we start Fiddler, open a browser and navigate to http://fineshoes.com/index.html, we can see the format of the HTTP request. It looks like this:

```
GET /index.html HTTP/1.1

Host: fineshoes.com
Connection: keep-alive
Cache-Control: max-age=0
Upgrade-Insecure-Requests: 1
User-Agent: Mozilla/5.0 (Windows NT 10.0; WOW64) AppleWebKit/537.36
    (KHTML, like Gecko) Chrome/52.0.2743.116 Safari/537.36
Accept: text/html,application/xhtml+xml,application/xml;q=0.9,*/*;q=0.8
Accept-Encoding: gzip, deflate, sdch
Accept-Language: en-US,en;q=0.8
```

The first line is called the request line and contains the HTTP verb used, which is GET in this case, the request URI /index.html, and the version of HTTP. The other lines are HTTP headers and their values, which are set by the browser. These capture things like the type of browser via the User-Agent line, whether the browser can accept gzipped responses via the Accept-Encoding line, and whether it's okay to reuse the TCP connection for multiple HTTP requests, indicated by the Connection line. In this section, we're only interested in the request line.

Suppose that we wanted our users to see /home in their browser's address bar instead of /index.html. However, since the Web servers still need to know the exact name of the file to serve, we wanted the servers to continue to see /index.html. Since HAProxy sits between the client and the servers, it's the perfect place to modify the message while it's in transit. We can use the `reqirep` directive to convert the old URI to the new one before it's forwarded on. Its syntax is:

```
reqirep <regex> <new string>
```

In the following example, we use `reqirep` to find the request within the HTTP request and replace it with our new string.

```
frontend mywebsite
  bind *:80
  reqirep ^(GET)\ /home\ (.*)    \1\ /index.html\ \2
  default_backend webservers
```

This will perform a case-insensitive search through all lines of the request, including the request line, trying to match each against the given regular expression `^(GET)\ /home\ (.*)`. Any matching lines will be replaced with the second parameter, `\1\ /index.html\ \2`. Our regular expression looks for a line that begins with GET, followed by a space, which we have to escape with a backslash so that HAProxy doesn't think we're starting a new parameter, and then `/home` followed by another escaped space, and then ending with any character any number of times as signified by `(.*)`.

Notice that the `(GET)` and the `(.*)` are surrounded by parentheses. These are called capture groups and they signify that, when we find a matching string, those parts of the match will be stored for later. We'll be able to recall those values and reuse them in our replacement string by referencing them with placeholder variables. For example, the variable `\1` would get a value of GET and the variable `\2` would get a value of HTTP/1.1.

When building your regular expressions, I recommend using the Regular Expressions 101 website at https://regex101.com. It is a good online sandbox for testing things out. Since we're using forward slashes in our URL, when using the regex101 website be sure to change the delimiter that starts and ends the expression to something other than that. HAProxy uses PCRE-style regular expressions.

The second parameter that we pass to `reqirep`, `\1\ /index.html\ \2`, is our new string. Here's where we use our capture groups to replace the `\1` and `\2` placeholders with the values from the original request line. So, it inserts GET for `\1` and HTTP/1.1 for `\2`. The middle of the regular expression `\ /home\`, is what we will replace. In our new string, it becomes `\ /index.html\`. That way, the request line will be changed from `GET /home HTTP/1.1` to `GET /index.html HTTP/1.1` for any user that navigates to http://fineshoes.com/home.

CHAPTER 10. CHANGING THE MESSAGE

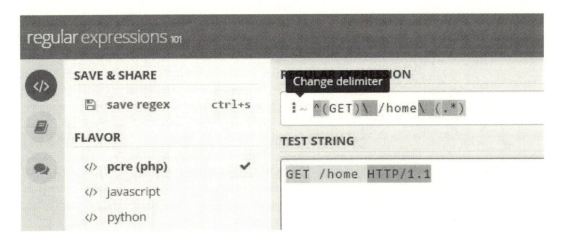

Figure 10.1: regex101.com

We can also use the following, slightly more cryptic regular expression to match on any HTTP verb such as GET, POST or PUT:

```
frontend mywebsite
  bind *:80
  reqirep ^([^\ :]*)\ /home\ (.*)    \1\ /index.html\ \2
  default_backend webservers
```

The client will see /home in their browser's address bar, but the server will see /index.html. Here's what gets logged by the NGINX Web server:

```
172.18.0.4 - - [24/Aug/2016:21:28:37 +0000] "GET /index.html HTTP/1.1"
    200 283 "-" "Mozilla/5.0 (Windows NT 10.0; WOW64) AppleWebKit/537.36
    (KHTML, like Gecko) Chrome/52.0.2743.116 Safari/537.36"
```

There is a caveat to using `reqirep`. If you are also redirecting clients to another domain by using a `redirect prefix` directive in the same `frontend`, then clients will see the URL change in their browser's address bar from /home to /index.html. To verify this, you could first update your hosts file so that both fineshoes.com and fantasticshoes.com map to your VM's IP address.

```
192.168.50.10 fineshoes.com
192.168.50.10 fantasticshoes.com
```

Using the following configuration, a client who requests http://fineshoes.com/home would be redirected to http://fantasticshoes.com/index.html.

```
frontend mywebsite
  bind *:80
  acl wantsfineshoes req.hdr(Host) -i -m str "fineshoes.com"
  redirect prefix http://fantasticshoes.com if wantsfineshoes
  reqirep ^(GET)\ /home\ (.*)     \1\ /index.html\ \2
  default_backend webservers
```

It doesn't matter whether the `reqirep` or the `redirect prefix` comes first. Client will see the URL change. If you absolutely do not want clients to see the modified URL, then you can move the `reqirep` directive to the `backend`. The following example would redirect users who request http://fineshoes.com/home to http://fantasticshoes.com/home.

```
frontend mywebsite
  bind *:80
  acl wantsfineshoes req.hdr(Host) -i -m str "fineshoes.com"
  redirect prefix http://fantasticshoes.com if wantsfineshoes
  default_backend webservers

backend webservers
  balance roundrobin
  reqirep ^(GET)\ /home\ (.*)     \1\ /index.html\ \2
  server web1 192.168.50.12:80 check
  server web2 192.168.50.13:80 check
```

This technique of rewriting the URL is also useful when we want to make two separate websites, which are perhaps controlled by two different departments within your company, appear unified. Suppose we had a website with the domain name blog.fineshoes.com that served up our company's blog. Now suppose that we wanted to make it so that instead of having users visit http://blog.fineshoes.com, we'd like for them visit http://fineshoes.com/blog. The first problem is that fineshoes.com doesn't know how to serve /blog. The second is that we need to route to a different domain, but only on the backend. Users should never see blog.fineshoes.com.

To solve the first problem, we'll use `reqirep` so that /blog is stripped off before it's sent to the servers. The second problem is solved by simply modifying the `server`

CHAPTER 10. CHANGING THE MESSAGE   143

directive in the `backend` to use blog.fineshoes.com as its destination. Up to now, we've only used IP addresses on the `server` line, but you can also use a domain name.

In the following example, we're using an `acl` to detect when the user has requesting /blog so that we can send them to the blog_servers `backend`. Our `server` directive sends requests to blog.fineshoes.com at port 80. However, that `backend` also has a `reqirep` directive that modifies the URL, replacing /blog with /.

```
frontend mywebsite
  bind *:80
  acl wantsblog path_beg /blog
  use_backend blog_servers if wantsblog
  default_backend webservers

backend blog_servers
  server blog1 blog.fineshoes.com:80 check
  reqirep ^([^\ :]*)\ /blog\ (.*)     \1\ /\ \2
```

Now when a user browses to http://fineshoes.com/blog, the backend will send it to http://blog.fineshoes.com/ and the request will be served correctly.

Adding request headers

Recall that an HTTP request looks like this:

```
GET / HTTP/1.1

Host:  fineshoes.com
Connection:  keep-alive
Cache-Control: max-age=0
Upgrade-Insecure-Requests: 1
User-Agent:  Mozilla/5.0 (Windows NT 10.0; WOW64) AppleWebKit/537.36
    (KHTML, like Gecko) Chrome/52.0.2743.116 Safari/537.36
Accept:  text/html,application/xhtml+xml,application/xml;q=0.9,*/*;q=0.8
Accept-Encoding:  gzip, deflate, sdch
Accept-Language:  en-US,en;q=0.8
```

CHAPTER 10. CHANGING THE MESSAGE

The browser adds headers, such as the ones we see here: Host, Connection, Cache-Control, and so on. When HAProxy intercepts the message, it can add more headers that the client will never know about. Only the backend server that fulfills the request will see them.

One use for this technique is to add a Via header so that the server knows that the request was routed through a proxy. In the following snippet, we set Via to the name of our frontend, mywebsite.

```
http-request set-header Via "%[req.hdr(Via)] mywebsite"
```

Since the Via header might have already been set by another proxy, we use %[req.hdr(Via)] to get the existing value before appending our own. Each value is separated by a space. The entire expression is surrounded by double quotes.

We can use Wireshark or tcpdump, which is a command-line packet analyzer available on Linux, to watch incoming requests and inspect their headers. Install tcpdump on the machine hosting your Web server with the following commands:

```
~$ sudo apt update
~$ sudo apt install tcpdump -y
```

Use the following tcpdump command to watch all GET requests on the eth1 network interface:

```
~$ sudo tcpdump -i eth1 -s 0 -A
    'tcp[((tcp[12:1] & 0xf0) >> 2):4] = 0x47455420'
```

You should see the Via header logged as you make requests to the website. You may have to monitor a different network interface, such as eth0 or lo, but it should appear at the end of the list of headers that were set by the browser.

```
GET / HTTP/1.1

Host: fineshoes.com
Cache-Control: max-age=0
Upgrade-Insecure-Requests: 1
User-Agent:  Mozilla/5.0 (Windows NT 10.0; WOW64) AppleWebKit/537.36
```

CHAPTER 10. CHANGING THE MESSAGE

```
    (KHTML, like Gecko) Chrome/52.0.2743.116 Safari/537.36
Accept:   text/html,application/xhtml+xml,application/xml;q=0.9,*/*;q=0.8
Accept-Encoding: gzip, deflate, sdch
Accept-Language: en-US,en;q=0.8
Via: mywebsite
```

We can set any header. The `http-request set-header` directive will overwrite the existing value if there is one. We can also control when to set the header by adding an `if` or `unless` parameter followed by a conditional statement. For example, we could add a header called X-Forwarded-Proto with a value of https only if the request came in over HTTPS. This is helpful if the request gets routed through several layers of proxies and the last one in line needs to know which protocol was originally used.

In the next example, we use the `ssl_fc` fetch method, which returns true when the request used HTTPS, to control when to add the X-Forwarded-Proto header.

```
listen mywebsite
  bind *:80
  bind *:443 ssl crt /etc/ssl/certs/mywebsite_cert.pem
  http-request set-header X-Forwarded-Proto https if { ssl_fc }
  server anotherproxy 192.168.50.15:80 check
```

When a request uses the HTTPS protocol, HAProxy will add the new header. The server will see it like this:

```
X-Forwarded-Proto https
```

Adding response headers

When our Web servers respond to a client's request, that response must flow back through HAProxy before it's ultimately sent to the client. This gives us the opportunity to append HTTP headers to the outgoing message. One use for this is to add a header that helps identify which server handled the request, for troubleshooting purposes.

Let's add a header called X-Served-By to the HTTP response by using the `http-response set-header` directive in the `backend`.

```
backend webservers
   server web1 192.168.50.30:80 check
   server web2 192.168.50.31:80 check
   server web3 192.158.50.32:80 check
   http-response set-header X-Served-By %[srv_id]
```

The `http-response set-header` directive sets the header, in this case X-Served-By, to the given value. I'm using the `srv_id` fetch method to get the numeric ID of the server that handled the request. When invoking a fetch method and getting its value, but not using it in an `acl`, surround it with square brackets and precede it with a percent sign, as in `%[srv_id]`.

Each `server` is assigned a numeric ID according to the order in which it appears in the configuration file. So, web1 gets an ID of 1, web2 gets 2, and web3 gets 3. Note that you can also explicitly set the ID with the `id` parameter, as in the following snippet where we assign the IDs 10, 20 and 30:

```
backend webservers
   server web1 192.168.50.30:80 check id 10
   server web2 192.168.50.31:80 check id 20
   server web3 192.158.50.32:80 check id 30
   http-response set-header X-Served-By %[srv_id]
```

We can use Fiddler to see the X-Served-By header in the response. Open Fiddler, make a request to your website and then view the Headers tab to see the response headers.

We can also add an `if` parameter so that a particular value is assigned to the header only when the given expression is true. In the following example, we set a more descriptive label for the X-Served-By header based on the value returned by the `srv_id` fetch method.

```
backend servers-http
   balance roundrobin
   server ray 192.168.50.30:80 check
   server egon 192.168.50.31:80 check
   server peter 192.168.50.32:80 check
   server winston 192.168.50.33:80 check
   http-response set-header X-Served-By ray if { srv_id eq 1 }
```

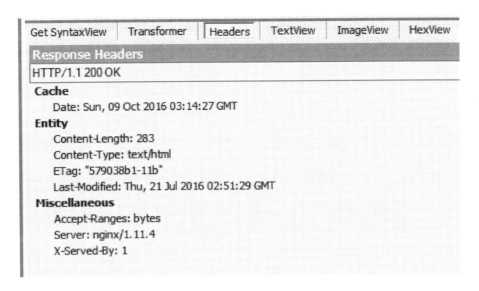

Figure 10.2: Response header in Fiddler

```
http-response set-header X-Served-By egon if { srv_id eq 2 }
http-response set-header X-Served-By peter if { srv_id eq 3 }
http-response set-header X-Served-By winston if { srv_id eq 4 }
```

The result, when the request is served by the first Web server, is that our header is set to ray.

According to the Open Web Application Security Project (OWASP), there are several response headers that are designed to improve the security of your website. Having HAProxy add them means they'll be added consistently to all responses. The first is the X-Frame-Options header. When set to sameorigin, another website cannot display your site within an HTML iframe. This prevents attacks like click-jacking.

```
http-response set-header X-Frame-Options sameorigin
```

Another security-related header is X-XSS-Protection, which enables cross-site-scripting (XSS) protection in some browsers including Internet Explorer and Chrome. Set its value to 1 and then set mode=block to drop any connection where XSS is detected.

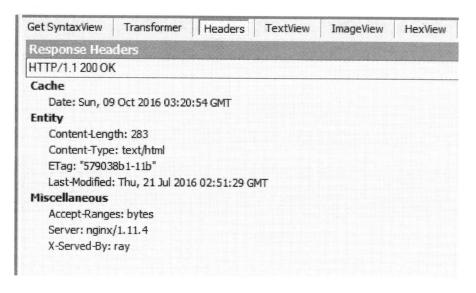

Figure 10.3: Descriptive labels

```
http-response set-header X-XSS-Protection "1; mode=block"
```

The X-Content-Type-Options header stops Internet Explorer and Chrome from trying to guess the content-type of a file and instead forces them to use the file's declared type. This prevents certain attacks where someone might try to upload a link to a discussion forum or user review that points to a file that's hosted on their own server, has an innocuous content-type like text/plain, but is actually executable JavaScript code. When this header is present, the browser will process the file as its declared content-type, text/plain, which renders it harmless. Set the header's value to nosniff.

```
http-response set-header X-Content-Type-Options nosniff
```

The Content-Security-Policy header lets you define which resources can be loaded into a page. You might, for example, only allow JavaScript files to be loaded if they come from your own domain or the https://ajax.googleapis.com CDN. Set it as follows:

```
http-response set-header Content-Security-Policy
    "script-src 'self' https://ajax.googleapis.com"
```

To test your website for missing security-related headers, try https://securityheaders.io. There you'll be able to scan your site and get a grade on how well you did.

Removing response headers

Many Web servers, including Apache and IIS, add HTTP headers to a response that describe the type of server it is and the kind of programming language or technology stack it's using. This doesn't really give us much benefit, but it could give an attacker enough information to spot a vulnerability. Quite a few security experts warn us that we should not be exposing so much information about our Web servers. We should remove these headers from all responses.

Two such headers are `Server` and `X-Powered-By`, which expose the type of server and the technology stack used. In the following example, it's clear that the server is Apache running PHP version 5.4.40.

```
Server: Apache/2.2.15 (Red Hat)
X-Powered-By: PHP/5.4.40
```

Here's one from an IIS Web server that also sends an `X-AspNet-Version` header:

```
Server: Microsoft-IIS/8.5
X-AspNet-Version: 4.0.30319
X-Powered-By: ASP.NET
```

We can have our proxy remove these headers by using the `http-response del-header` directive.

```
frontend mywebsite
  bind *:80
  default_backend webservers
  http-response del-header Server
  http-response del-header X-Powered-By
  http-response del-header X-AspNet-Version
```

Now, all responses will have these headers removed before being sent back to the client. That's not to say that the technology or server we're using couldn't be discovered in some other way, but at least we're not giving it away for free.

Compressing outgoing files with gzip

When it comes to compressing files with gzip, you've got a decision to make: Have each of your Web servers do it or have HAProxy handle it all. The original intent of compression was to minimize each file and thus maximize network bandwidth so that you could receive and respond to more HTTP requests. Typically, however, the cost of compression on CPU means that the Web server can't process as many requests as quickly anyway, so some of the benefit is cancelled out.

This is especially true for websites that must use their CPU cycles to generate dynamic content, such as when using ASP.NET or Java. Some interesting charts about this can be found on Web Performance, Inc.'s website at http://www.webperformance.com/library/reports/moddeflate. Web Performance states that when a server generates large files dynamically, compressing those files on the server can actually make performance worse.

Doing the compression somewhere other than the Web server means that we can get the benefit of reduced file sizes without canibalizing the server's CPU that it needs to process requests. HAProxy can do this work. However, it means that the load balancer is going to have to handle more processing itself. It would have to be a more powerful machine.

To enable gzip compression in HAProxy, add the `compression algo` directive to the `backend` that contains your Web servers. In the following example, we compress HTML, CSS and JavaScript files that are returned from our web1 and web2 servers. You should know that there are certain types of files that you don't want to compress. These include images, videos and PDFs because they're a binary format that is already compressed. Using gzip on them might actually make them bigger!

```
backend webservers
  mode http
  server web1 192.168.50.12:80 check
  server web2 192.168.50.13:80 check
  compression algo gzip
  compression type text/html text/css text/javascript
    application/javascript
```

The `compression algo` directive sets the compression algorithm to use. At this time, gzip is the only good option. The `compression type` directive sets which

MIME types to compress. Here I've specified that I'd like to compress HTML, CSS and JavaScript files only.

If the backend server has already gzip compressed the files, HAProxy will notice and won't compress them again. You can also have HAProxy remove the Accept-Encoding header from all incoming requests. That's the header that states whether the browser can accept gzip-compressed files. If we remove it before it reaches the backend server, the server won't try to compress the files even if it's enabled to do so. That way, HAProxy will assume full responsibility for compression. Do this by adding the `compression offload` directive, like so:

```
compression algo gzip
compression type text/html text/css text/javascript application/javascript
compression offload
```

When using `compression offload`, be sure that the machine where HAProxy is running is powerful enough to handle the extra work.

Device detection with 51Degrees

51Degrees is a company that makes a software library that inspects HTTP headers, such as User-Agent, to determine what sort of device, such as desktop, mobile phone or tablet, that the client is using. It then adds new HTTP request headers containing this information. To enable it in HAProxy version 1.6, we'll have to build HAProxy from its source code. We'll demonstrate this on Ubuntu 16.04.

Start out by SSH'ing into your Ubuntu machine and downloading the 51Degrees source code from its GitHub repository. Save it to /usr/local/src. The following snippet installs git first.

```
~$ sudo apt update
~$ sudo apt install git -y
~$ cd /usr/local/src
~$ sudo git clone https://github.com/51Degrees/Device-Detection
```

This will create a directory called Device-Detection. The files that are particularly interesting are in the Device-Detection/src/pattern and Device-Detection/data directories. The pattern directory contains the source code files that define the 51Degrees functionality. The data directory contains a DAT file, 51Degrees-LiteV3.2.dat,

CHAPTER 10. CHANGING THE MESSAGE

that contains the rules for parsing incoming HTTP headers to see which sort of device the client is using. This includes the free rules, also known as the Lite tier. More rules come with the paid versions. You can learn more about each tier at https://51degrees.com/resources/property-dictionary.

To integrate 51Degrees with HAProxy, we'll need to compile HAProxy from scratch, adding in the necessary 51Degrees flags. Since there's an apt package for HAProxy already, it's easiest to install that first and then replace the executable with our freshly compiled one. That way, boilerplate files like the init.d script will be set up for us.

The commands for installing HAProxy via apt are as follows:

```
~$ sudo add-apt-repository ppa:vbernat/haproxy-1.6
~$ sudo apt update
~$ sudo apt install haproxy -y
```

Next download the HAProxy source code. Use `wget` to download the tarball and then the `tar` command to unzip it.

```
~$ cd /usr/local/src
~$ sudo wget http://www.haproxy.org/download/1.6/src/haproxy-1.6.4.tar.gz
~$ sudo tar -zxvf haproxy-1.6.4.tar.gz
~$ sudo rm -f haproxy-1.6.4.tar.gz
~$ cd haproxy-1.6.4
```

We need to install a few packages needed to build HAProxy: build-essential for the C compiler, libpcre3 for Perl-compatible regular expressions, and libssl for OpenSSL support. We can install all three with a single apt install command:

```
~$ sudo apt install build-essential libpcre3 libpcre3-dev libssl-dev -y
```

Make sure that you're in the /usr/local/src/haproxy-1.6.4 directory and then set the compilation flags to use during the build: The `USE_51DEGREES` flag enables device detection and `51DEGREES_SRC` points to the pattern directory.

```
~$ sudo make TARGET=linux2628 USE_OPENSSL=1 USE_PCRE=1
       USE_ZLIB=1 USE_51DEGREES=1
       51DEGREES_SRC=/usr/local/src/Device-Detection/src/pattern
```

CHAPTER 10. CHANGING THE MESSAGE

Build the project:

~$ `sudo make install`

Stop the existing HAProxy service:

~$ `sudo service haproxy stop`

Replace the existing HAProxy executable with the newly compiled one:

~$ `sudo cp /usr/local/sbin/haproxy /usr/sbin`

Now we can edit the /etc/haproxy/haproxy.cfg configuration file so that it has the settings for 51Degrees. In the `global` section, we'll add four new directives: `51degrees-data-file`, which sets the path to the DAT file, `51degrees-property-name-list`, which lists all of the device-detection rules that we want to use, `51degrees-property-separator`, which specifies the character used to separate multiple values in the device-detection headers we'll add, and `51degrees-cache-size`, which turns on caching and sets how many previous detection results to cache.

```
51degrees-data-file
  /usr/local/src/Device-Detection/data/51Degrees-LiteV3.2.dat
51degrees-property-name-list IsMobile GeoLocation TouchEvents
51degrees-property-separator ,
51degrees-cache-size   10000
```

The next thing to do is add `http-request set-header` directives to the `frontend` section where we want to capture device information. We can add as many new headers as we want, with any names that we want. Use the `51d.all` fetch method to get the value for the given rule. Here's an example that creates three new HTTP request headers to send to the backend Web server that declare whether the device is a mobile phone, whether it supports geo-location, and whether it has touch capabilities.

```
frontend mywebsite
  bind *:80
  default_backend webservers
  http-request set-header X-51D-IsMobile %[51d.all(IsMobile)]
  http-request set-header X-51D-SupportsGeolocation %[51d.all(GeoLocation)]
  http-request set-header X-51D-SupportsTouch %[51d.all(TouchEvents)]
```

We can also combine up to five values into one header. They'll be separated by the character defined by the **51degrees-property-separator** directive. Here's an example that combines our previous rules into a single request header called X-51D-MobileGeoTouch:

```
http-request set-header X-51D-MobileGeoTouch
    %[51d.all(IsMobile,SupportsGeolocation,SupportsTouch)]
```

Last, restart the HAProxy service.

```
~$ sudo service haproxy start
```

That's it. When we make requests to our website, we should see the new requests headers included. A helpful tool for monitoring incoming requests is tcpdump, which prints incoming requests to the console. It's similar to WireShark, but without the GUI. After we've installed a Web server such as NGINX onto another virtual machine, we can SSH in and install tcpdump like so:

```
~$ sudo apt update
~$ sudo apt install tcpdump -y
```

The following tcpdump command will print requests along with their headers that are captured on the eth1 network interface:

```
~$ sudo tcpdump -i eth1 -s 0 -A 'tcp[((tcp[12:1] & 0xf0) >> 2):4]
    = 0x47455420'
```

The request headers that the Web server sees will look like the following:

Figure 10.4: Device emulation in Chrome

```
X-51D-IsMobile: False
X-51D-SupportsGeoLocation: True
X-51D-SupportsTouch: True
```

In order to emulate various devices, we can use Google Chrome's Developer Tools.

It has a menu for impersonating phones and tablets. In Chrome, press **F12** and then click the Toggle device toolbar button at the top. It looks like a phone icon. Refresh the page and you'll see the headers change.

You website is now free to look for these headers and enable features based on them.

Summary

In this chapter, we learned how to alter requests and responses as they flow through HAProxy. We were able to change the URL by using the `reqirep` directive and regular expressions. This is a powerful technique that lets us show the server a URL that's different from the one that the client sees.

We also saw how to add HTTP headers to requests and responses. Doing this at the load balancer means the work will be done consistently. We also learned how to remove certain headers from responses for better security.

We enabled gzip compression, but noted that whether this will be optimal for you depends on how powerful the machine where your load balancer is running is. Last, we added support for detecting the type of device the client is using by recompiling HAProxy with 51Degrees and adding specialized headers to the request.

Chapter 11

Security

HAProxy is the gateway that all traffic passes through before it reaches your backend servers. For that reason, we should try to harden it against hackers and think of it as a first line of defense. Although it doesn't have a built-in firewall or other dedicated security layer, it can thwart some basic attacks.

In this chapter, we'll cover the following topics:

- Running HAProxy in a chrooted directory
- Enabling Basic authentication
- Preventing clients from opening too many connections
- Defending against slow HTTP requests
- Rate limiting users
- Denying an attacker for a time
- Whitelisting certain IP addresses

Running HAProxy in a chroot

When you install HAProxy through your system's package manager, it will typically already be configured to run in a Linux chroot. Chroot, which is short for change root directory, is a Linux command that changes what a running process perceives to be the root directory of the filesystem. So, instead of seeing the true filesystem and having access to it all, it would only see the contents of the folder you select.

Daemons that regularly allow people to connect to them are often chrooted: FTP servers, Web servers, SSH sessions, etc. This gives us some protection against a hacker who finds a way to run arbitrary commands within the process, such as injecting code that gives them a shell prompt and then lets them wreaks havoc on the server. As far as security measures go, confining a process to a particular directory doesn't guarantee that a clever hacker couldn't escape. However, it does make it harder for them and is a decent first defense.

We should not run a process that we want to chroot as the root user because root can escape the directory. So, let's create a new user to run the HAProxy process as. We'll call it haproxy_user and add it to a group with the same name.

```
~$ sudo groupadd haproxy_user
~$ sudo useradd -g haproxy_user haproxy_user
```

Next, create the directory to confine the HAProxy process to by using the `mkdir` command. I'll call the directory haproxy_jail and place it under /var.

```
~$ sudo mkdir /var/haproxy_jail
```

Make sure that the haproxy_jail directory is only writable by root by using the `chmod` command, like so:

```
~$ sudo chmod 755 /var/haproxy_jail
```

If you'll need to access any files outside of /var/haproxy_jail, such as TLS certificates under /etc/ssl/certs or /dev/log for syslog logging, then you'll need to `mount` them to the chrooted directory. This will make that folder visible to the running process. In the following snippet, we mount the /dev/log and /etc/ssl/certs folder within our chrooted directory, /var/haproxy_jail:

```
~$ cd /var/haproxy_jail
~$ sudo mkdir dev
~$ sudo mount --bind /dev /var/haproxy_jail/dev
~$ sudo mkdir certs
~$ sudo mount --bind /etc/ssl/certs /var/haproxy_jail/certs
```

CHAPTER 11. SECURITY

Next, open /etc/haproxy/haproxy.cfg and add a `chroot` directive to the `global` section. It should point to our /var/haproxy_jail directory. Also, add a `user` and `group` directive that specify the user and group that HAProxy should run as. The `daemon` directive runs HAProxy as a background process.

```
global
  chroot /var/haproxy_jail
  user haproxy_user
  group haproxy_user
  daemon
```

Then restart the HAProxy service.

```
~$ sudo service haproxy restart
```

To check if the HAProxy process has been chroot'ed, view the running processes by using `ps` and then filter for haproxy with `grep`:

```
~$ ps auxwww | grep haproxy
```

You will see the HAProxy process and its process ID (PID). In the following example, the PID is 2253.

```
haproxy   2253  0.0  0.1  37768  5500 ?   S    19:01   0:00
    /usr/sbin/haproxy -f /etc/haproxy/haproxy.cfg -p /run/haproxy.pid -Ds
```

Using that PID number, navigate to the directory under /proc that has the same number. So, in our example, we'd navigate to the /proc/2253 directory.

```
~$ cd /proc/2253
```

Check to see what the root directory for this process is by using the `ls` command with the arguments `-lad root`. You should see that it is, as HAProxy sees it, the folder that you specified for the `chroot` directive in the haproxy.cfg file.

```
~$ sudo ls -lad root
lrwxrwxrwx 1 root root 0 Jun 17 19:02 root -> /var/haproxy_jail
```

If it isn't chrooted, we'll see the root directory set to /, as in the following snippet:

```
~$ sudo ls -lad root
lrwxrwxrwx 1 root root 0 Jun 17 19:02 root -> /
```

Enabling basic authentication

If you need a simple mechanism for limiting access to a proxied website, Basic authentication may be the answer. Basic authentication prompts each visitor for a username and password and matches the supplied values against lists defined in the /etc/haproxy/haproxy.cfg file. The main advantage of this is that it's easy to implement. The major drawback, as we'll discuss in a moment, is that the credentials are sent over the wire without encryption, making it possible for eavesdroppers to view them.

Configure Basic authentication by adding a new section called `userlist` to the /etc/haproxy/haproxy.cfg file. In the following example, we define a list of usernames and passwords in a `userlist` section that I've decided to call TrustedPeople:

```
userlist TrustedPeople
   user bob insecure-password password123
   user alice insecure-password anotherpassword
```

Each username/password combination is set with a `user` directive. In this case, we have two users: bob and alice. To store their passwords, use the `insecure-password` parameter followed by a string. Note that these are not Linux users and they don't map to any profiles on the system. They only exist in this configuration file.

I mentioned that Basic authentication does not safeguard the secrecy of the usernames or passwords. The credentials, as they pass between the client and HAProxy are sent in the clear. The client's browser Base64 encodes them and sends them in an HTTP header called Authorization. This makes it possible for someone sniffing network traffic to view this information. Therefore, to encrypt the data while it's in transit, we'll enable TLS termination in the proxy where we want authentication.

Add a `bind` statement that listens on port 443 to your `frontend` or `listen` section and add the `ssl` and `crt` parameters to enable TLS termination. We'll also add a `redirect scheme` directive to redirect all HTTP traffic to HTTPS.

CHAPTER 11. SECURITY

```
userlist TrustedPeople
  user bob insecure-password password123
  user alice insecure-password anotherpassword

frontend mywebsite
  bind *:80
  bind *:443 ssl crt /etc/ssl/certs/site.pem
  redirect scheme https if !{ ssl_fc }
  default_backend webservers
```

Next, add `http-request auth` to any `backend` where you'd like to use Basic authentication. We do this in the `backend` so that the scheme will have been converted to HTTPS before it gets there. We also need to add an `if` or `unless` statement to the `http-request auth` directive so that the user is only asked to log in if they have not already done so. The `http_auth` fetch method returns true if the user is already authenticated, based on the given `userlist`.

```
backend webservers
  balance roundrobin
  http-request auth unless { http_auth(TrustedPeople) }
  server web1 192.168.50.11:80 check
  server web2 192.168.50.12:80 check
```

Now users will be prompted to enter a username and password before they can access the site.

We can also encrypt the passwords that are stored in the haproxy.cfg file. The `mkpasswd` command will encrypt our password, but first, we have to install it. It comes included in the whois package.

```
~$ sudo apt install whois
```

The following command will encrypt the password, mypassword123, with SHA-256:

```
~$ mkpasswd -m sha-256 mypassword123
$5$11J/5f1641$IK6c68Nvn6EGYw6E/Y.R5/Ekxhe577M4J5msno
```

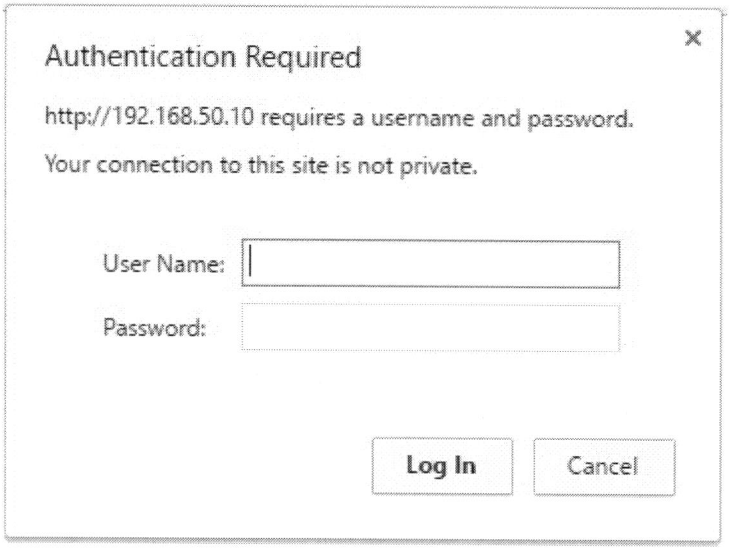

Figure 11.1: Basic Authentication prompt

Then, update the user directive so that it uses the password parameter instead of insecure-password and include the encrypted value.

```
userlist TrustedPeople
  user bob password $5$11J/5f1641$IK6c68Nvn6EGYw6E/Y.R5/Ekxhe577M4J5msno
```

When the website prompts for a username and password, we'd still give bob and password123. Note that encrypting the password in the configuration file will not encrypt it in the HTTP message. It's still important to enable HTTPS.

Preventing too many parallel connections

One of the simplest ways that an attacker could try to use up many resources on a server, causing a denial-of-service condition, is to open many simultaneous TCP connections. Although a Web server can typically handle a large number of connections, serving them takes memory and CPU, especially if the attacker requests dynamic webpages that requires a lot of processing. To mitigate this, we can put a limit on the number of active connections a single user is allowed to have.

CHAPTER 11. SECURITY

We need to be careful about this because a webpage may legitimately have many image, CSS and JavaScript resources to serve. To fetch these files faster, a browser will open several connections in parallel. The HTTP 1.1 specification suggests that browsers should open no more than two connections at a time to any particular host. However, this isn't followed by most browsers, which will open six or seven connections at once. However, a client that opens more than that, say ten or twenty, is likely malicious.

Note that you should be mindful of whether some of your clients are connecting using a shared IP address, which will inflate the number of connections they have. In that case, we can whitelist them, as we'll see later on. However, connections are usually opened and closed within a few milliseconds, so even this may not be necessary.

In the following snippet, we check whether the client has more than 10 connections open. If so, we reject their connection attempts, returning a 403 Forbidden.

```
frontend mywebsite
  bind *:80
  stick-table type ip  size 100k  expire 30s  store conn_cur
  http-request track-sc0 src
  acl too_many_connections src_conn_cur ge 10
  http-request deny if too_many_connections
  default_backend webservers
```

The `stick-table` directive creates a storage where we can associate each client's source IP address with their number of concurrent connections. The `http-request track-sc0 src` line adds each request to the table and uses the client's source IP as the key. The `store conn_cur` parameter on the `stick-table` adds the current number of connections, updating the entry in the table each time a new request comes through.

Next, we define a rule, using the `acl` directive, that checks how many connections that client has by reading it from the table via the `src_conn_cur` fetch method. The `ge` parameter means greater-than and is how we set our limit to be no more than ten at a time. If the client has more than or equal to ten active connections, the too_many_connections rule is set to true. Note that the `acl` is not evaluated until we use it in the following `http-request deny` directive. Until then, it's just inactive code.

The second `http-request` directive uses the `deny` parameter to reject any incoming connection that meets the given criteria, which in this case is our too_many_connections rule. The client will receive an HTTP 403 Forbidden response until their number of connections drops below the threshold.

One way to test that this configuration works is by downloading the free tool Fiddler from http://www.telerik.com/fiddler. Using Fiddler, you can replay a request to your site multiple times to simulate having many open connections at once. After a certain amount, you should start to see your requests rejected.

Defending against HTTP slow requests

In this section, we'll talk about defending your website against a denial-of-service attack called Slowloris. This attack involves the client intentionally sending an HTTP request very slowly so that it never times out, but never finishes either. With enough of those kinds of requests hogging a Web server's pool of threads, legitimate users won't be able to connect.

First, let's go into some background. When a client makes a request to our website, they connect to a TCP port, usually port 80, on the Web server. Then they send a stream of bytes over that connection that follow a predefined format for an HTTP request message. The first bytes to come across are the HTTP headers. If the client never starts sending these bytes, then we can consider the client unresponsive and kill the connection after a certain amount of time. This is controlled with the `timeout client` directive in the `defaults` section.

```
defaults
  timeout client 10s
```

It is important that you set this directive, as without it, inactive connections would build up until HAProxy couldn't accept any more. You'll even get a warning from HAProxy telling you that your configuration is bad:

> [WARNING] 175/013237 (6) : config : missing timeouts for frontend 'mywebsite'. While not properly invalid, you will certainly encounter various problems with such a configuration. To fix this, please ensure that all following timeouts are set to a non-zero value: 'client', 'connect', 'server'.

CHAPTER 11. SECURITY

mywebsite																		
	Queue			Session rate			Sessions					Bytes		Denied		Errors		
	Cur	Max	Limit	Cur	Max	Limit	Cur	Max	Limit	Total	LbTot	Last	In	Out	Req	Resp	Req	Conn	Resp
Frontend				0	48	-	401	401	2 000	401			10 488	340 174	0	0	0		

webservers																				
	Queue			Session rate			Sessions						Bytes		Denied		Errors		Warnings	
	Cur	Max	Limit	Cur	Max	Limit	Cur	Max	Limit	Total	LbTot	Last	In	Out	Req	Resp	Req	Conn	Resp	Retr	Redi
web1	0	0		0	0		0	0	-	0	0	?	0	0		0		0	0	0	
web2	0	0	-	0	0		0	0	-	0	0	?	0	0		0		0	0	0	
Backend	0	0		0	0		0	0	200	0	0	?	0	0		0		0	0	0	

Figure 11.2: Buffering slowloris

While `timeout client` protects us from connections that don't send any data, a hacker may take a different approach: Sending the headers very slowly. That way, the connection won't be cut off due to inactivity, but it ties up the server's resources indefinitely. This kind of attack is called Slowloris. The attacker hopes that by opening enough of these slow-moving connections, the server will run out of threads to service legitimate requests.

Out-of-the-box, we get some protection against Slowloris. HAProxy doesn't forward a request to our backend servers until it has the entire message. Until then, it buffers the bytes on its end. This is good for our Web servers, since HAProxy can buffer a lot more requests than a server like IIS or Apache can. The HAProxy Stats page looks like the following when HAProxy is buffering many slow-moving requests, but correctly not passing them to the backend server:

We can go even further though. By adding a `timeout http-request` directive to the `defaults` section, HAProxy will kill any request that doesn't send all of its headers within the specified amount of time. In the following snippet, we set it to five seconds. That should be more than enough time for normal users, even those with slow connections, to send the full request.

```
defaults
  timeout client 10s
  timeout http-request 5s
```

Now the Stats page shows that the long-running connections are killed. These are reported as requests that had Errors.

At this point, we're protected against Slowloris attacks, but there's something else an attacker can try: Sending a POST request where the HTTP headers are sent at normal speed, but the body of the POST is sent very slowly. This variation on

CHAPTER 11. SECURITY

Figure 11.3: Killing slowloris

Figure 11.4: Slow Post

Slowloris is called an R-U-Dead-Yet attack. Version 1.6 of HAProxy won't detect this and will pass the slow-moving requests on to the backend servers. You can see this in the following Stats page:

To defend against R-U-Dead-Yet attacks, we can add an `option http-buffer-request` directive to the `defaults` section. This includes the time taken to send the message body in the `http-request` timeout.

```
defaults
  timeout client 10s
  timeout http-request 5s
  option http-buffer-request
```

The Stats page now shows that the backend servers are once again protected.

ProactiveRISK makes a tool called Switchblade that will diagnose if you are vulnerable to these attacks. It can be found at the website:

https://sites.google.com/a/proactiverisk.com/pr2/home/proactivetools.

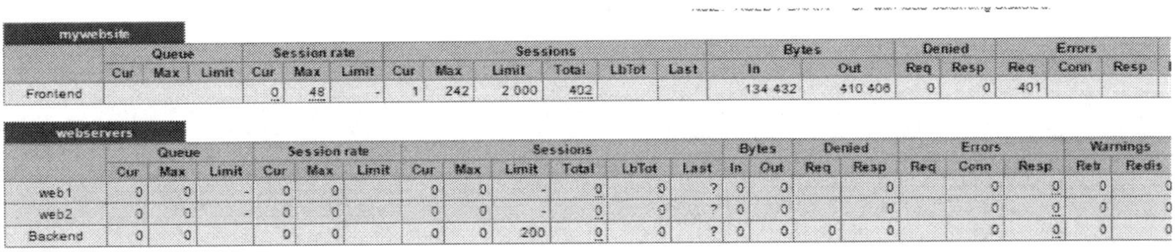

CHAPTER 11. SECURITY

mywebsite	Queue			Session rate			Sessions					Bytes		Denied		Errors		
	Cur	Max	Limit	Cur	Max	Limit	Cur	Max	Limit	Total	LbTot	Last	In	Out	Req	Resp	Req	Conn	Resp
Frontend				0	48	-	1	242	2 000	402			134 432	410 406	0	0	401		

webservers	Queue			Session rate			Sessions					Bytes		Denied		Errors		Warnings	
	Cur	Max	Limit	Cur	Max	Limit	Cur	Max	Limit	Total	LbTot	Last	In	Out	Req	Resp	Req	Conn	Resp	Retr	Redis
web1	0	0	-	0	0		0	0	-	0	0	?	0	0		0		0	0	0	0
web2	0	0	-	0	0		0	0	-	0	0	?	0	0		0		0	0	0	0
Backend	0	0		0	0		0	0	200	0	0	?	0	0		0		0	0	0	0

Figure 11.5: Slow Post protection

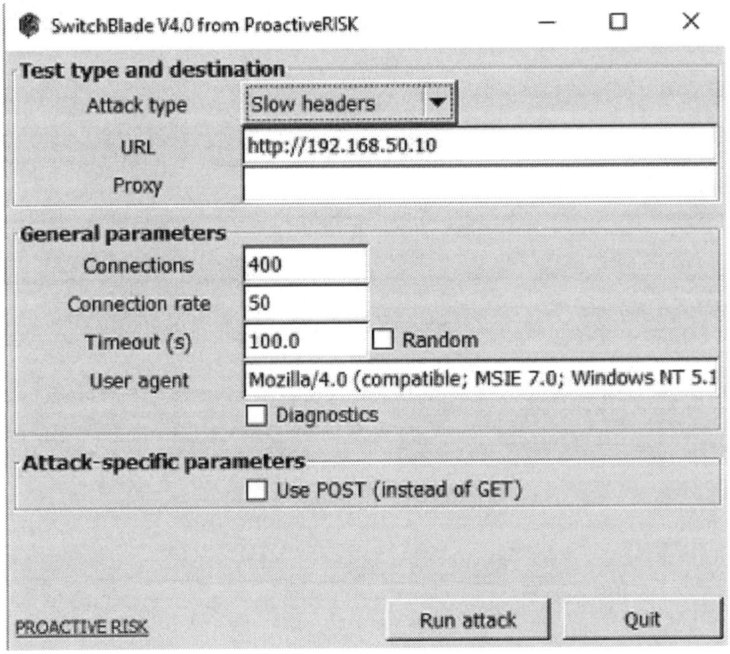

Figure 11.6: ProactiveRISK Switchblade

It has options for executing Slowloris and R-U-Dead-Yet attacks against your website. You might also try the slowloris.py command-line tool from https://github.com/gkbrk/slowloris.

Rate limiting

Rate limiting means allowing clients to only use a certain amount of your website's bandwidth. When they exceed a threshold, we begin to limit their use. This safeguards us against malicious users who intend to hog bandwidth in order to prevent other users from accessing the site. In this section, we'll learn how to limit users based on three things:

- The number of connections they've opened over a given time
- The number of bytes they've downloaded within a given time
- The number of HTTP requests they've sent over a given time

Let's look at the first scenario. A user who opens many connections over a short time may consume all our server's available threads, or at least enough to slow down other users. We can use a `stick-table` that stores the `conn_rate` data type to track each client's connection rate. It will look like this:

```
stick-table type ip  size 200k  expire 30s  store conn_rate(3s)
```

The HAProxy documentation at:

- http://cbonte.github.io/haproxy-dconv/1.6/configuration.html

describes `conn_rate` in the following way:

> It reports the average incoming connection rate over that period, in connections per period.

CHAPTER 11. SECURITY

The last part, connections per period, is what we should pay attention to. The `conn_rate` type simply counts a client's open connections that were created within the time period. So, it's less of an average and more of a count within a time period. For example, if a client opens five connections within three seconds, their connection rate would be five.

I like to set the time period to something small, like three seconds, as in the previous example. That way, it's easy to say something like, The client should not open more than 20 connections per second, which equates to 60 connections over three seconds. If a client manages to open 60 connections within that time, we can assume it's not normal behavior.

In the following example, we track each client's connection rate by using the `conn_rate` data type on a `stick-table`. If their connection rate goes above 60, we use the `http-request deny` directive to reject their requests and return 403 Forbidden responses until their connection rate drops down again.

```
frontend mywebsite
  bind *:80
  default_backend webservers
  stick-table type ip  size 200k  expire 30s  store conn_rate(3s)
  http-request track-sc0 src
  http-request deny if { sc0_conn_rate ge 60 }
```

First we create a `stick-table` to keep track of each user by their source IP address. Each IP will be associated with its connection rate because we've appended the `store` parameter with the `conn_rate` data type. Note that the `expire` parameter determines how long a record will be kept in the table and should be at least twice as long as the period. Next, the `http-request track-sc0 src` line starts tracking each client by their IP. Each entry that's added to the table is immediately associated with the client's connection rate. The `http-request deny` directive uses the `sc0_conn_rate` fetch method to get the client's connection rate from the `stick-table` and rejects anyone who opens more than 60 connections during the time period of three seconds.

We can also rate limit the client by the amount of data that they're downloading. This is useful when you're hosting an API that returns large amounts of data in its responses or if you're serving large files such as PDFs. Rate limiting this will prevent a single user from monopolizing your bandwidth.

In the following example, we limit each user to 10,000,000 bytes (10MB) of downloads within 60 seconds. If they go over that, their requests will be refused. For the sake of learning, I'm storing both the connection rate with the `conn_rate` data type and the download rate with the `bytes_out_rate` in the same `stick-table`. We could, of course, only capture one or the other.

```
frontend mywebsite
  bind *:80
  default_backend webservers
  stick-table type ip size 200k expire 120s store conn_rate(3s),
    bytes_out_rate(60s)
  http-request track-sc0 src
  http-request deny if { sc0_conn_rate gt 60 }
  http-request deny if { sc0_bytes_out_rate gt 10000000 }
```

Now, if we host a 2MB PDF file on our server and then try to download it more than five times within 60 seconds, our requests will be denied. We can also rate limit the number of bytes uploaded. For that, use the `bytes_in_rate` data type. Then use `sc0_bytes_in_rate` to get the value back. This can protect you from users trying to upload too much too fast.

In the last part of this section, we'll take a look at limiting users based on the number of HTTP requests that they send. We'll use the `http_req_rate` data type on the `stick-table` to track the number of HTTP requests a client makes over the given time period. Then we get this value using the `sc0_http_req_rate` fetch method.

```
frontend mywebsite
  bind *:80
  default_backend webservers
  stick-table type ip  size 200k  expire 30s  store http_req_rate(3s)
  http-request track-sc0 src
  http-request deny if { sc0_http_req_rate ge 60 }
```

Like we did with connection rate limiting, we reject clients who send more than 60 requests within three seconds. This equals 20 requests per second. You'll want to adjust the threshold based on how many files your webpages serve and how fast your response time is.

Denying requests from an attacker for a time

When we detect that a user may be abusing our website, we can deny their requests for a certain amount of time. We'll build on the example where we tracked each client's connection rate. In the following snippet, when a client's connection rate is too high, we flag them as an abuser and deny their requests for two minutes.

```
frontend mywebsite
  bind *:80
  default_backend webservers
  stick-table type ip  size 200k  expire 2m  store conn_rate(3s),gpc0
  acl conn_rate_abuse sc0_conn_rate gt 60
  acl flag_as_abuser sc0_inc_gpc0 gt 0
  acl is_abuser src_get_gpc0 gt 0
  http-request track-sc0 src
  http-request deny if is_abuser
  http-request deny if conn_rate_abuse flag_as_abuser
```

First, we define a `stick-table` that uses the `store` parameter to save two types of data: the client's connection rate, via the `conn_rate` data type, and the `gpc0` data type, which is a counter where we can store a zero or a one to indicate that the client has been flagged. This flag is the key to denying a user's requests. When we've flagged somebody, we don't have to keep checking their connection rate. We already know that they've tripped our alarms.

Next we set up three `acl` rules: The first checks if the connection rate is too high, as discussed in the previous section; the second uses the `sc0_inc_gpc0` fetch method to increment the `gpc0` counter to one; and the third uses the `src_get_gpc0` fetch method to get that flag from the `stick-table` and check whether it's greater than zero.

Let's talk about those last two a little more. The flag_as_abuser `acl`, when it is evaluated, increments our counter. This flags the associated client so that we will remember to deny their requests. In the same breath, it checks whether the counter is greater than zero. This will, of course, be true, since we just incremented the counter. An `acl` has to return true or false. That's why we've tacked that `gt 0` onto the end of the line.

```
acl flag_as_abuser sc0_inc_gpc0 gt 0
```

CHAPTER 11. SECURITY

Note that this rule is only evaluated, and hence the counter incremented, when and if the conn_rate_abuse rule is true. Consider the following line:

`http-request deny if conn_rate_abuse flag_as_abuser`

You would read this as deny if conn_rate_abuse is true AND flag_as_abuser is true. If conn_rate_abuse is false, the second condition, flag_as_abuser will not be evaluated, due to short-circuit evaluation. So, we only flag them when their connection rate is high.

The last `acl`, is_abuser, uses the `src_get_gpc0` to get the counter's value. It returns true if the counter is greater than zero.

`acl is_abuser src_get_gpc0 gt 0`

We check this on every request to see whether the client has been flagged via the following line:

`http-request deny if is_abuser`

When an `http-request deny` directive rejects a request, no other lines are evaluated. Also remember that `acl` directives are inactive until something such as an `http-request deny` uses them. So, the `acl` directive does nothing on its own.

So what controls how long to deny a client? On the `stick-table` directive, there's an `expire` parameter. That's what determines how long a record will exist in the table and guarantees that the client will be denied for the specified length of time. In this case, I've set it to two minutes. However, `expire` only begins counting once there is no activity from the client. If the client continues making requests, the timeout will keep being reset and the client will be denied for, possibly, forever. The client must stop making requests and let the two minutes expire before they'll be allowed access.

Denying a request returns a 403 Forbidden response to the client. If you would prefer to stop processing their requests without letting them know, replace **deny** with **silent-drop**. The client will see a request that seems to take forever to get a response.

`http-request silent-drop if is_abuser`

When you start rejecting clients, be sure to collect information about who is being affected. HAProxy captures this when it returns a 403 response in its syslog logs. In some cases, you may want to whitelist certain users, as we'll discuss in the next section.

Whitelisting IP addresses

In some cases, you may want to allow a set of IP addresses that are whitelisted to always be accepted, even if they trigger rules that would have otherwise denied them. In the following example, we store the client's error rate in a `stick-table` by using the `http_err_rate` data type. If, over a sampled time of five seconds, the client receives more than 10 errors, such as HTTP 404 Not Found, then we flag them as an abuser and deny them until the record in the table expires. We've set the expiration time to two minutes.

```
frontend mywebsite
  bind *:80
  stick-table type ip  size 200k  expire 2m  store http_err_rate(5s),gpc0
  acl too_many_errors src_http_err_rate gt 10
  acl flag_as_abuser sc0_inc_gpc0 gt 0
  acl is_abuser src_get_gpc0 gt 0
  acl whitelisted src 10.0.0.0/8 172.16.0.0/12 192.168.0.0/16
  http-request track-sc0 src
  http-request allow if whitelisted
  http-request deny if is_abuser
  http-request deny if too_many_errors flag_as_abuser
  default_backend webservers
```

The client's error rate is tracked automatically whenever we see their IP address because we've associated the `http_err_rate` data type with the `stick-table`. The line `http-request track-sc0 src` adds the client's IP address into the stick table. We then define an `acl` called too_many_errors that calls the `src_http_err_rate` fetch method to check whether the client's error rate is greater than 10.

```
acl too_many_errors src_http_err_rate gt 10
```

A client will often show a high error rate when they are scanning your website for vulnerabilities. A scan often tries to access files that have well-known names, such as admin.php. This can produce a lot of File Not Found responses. A normal user might stumble upon one of these every now and then, but to get 10 within five seconds is certainly something that deserves to trip alarms.

The `stick-table` in this example tracks the `gpc0` data type in addition to the error rate. This is a simple counter that, when incremented to one, flags the client as an abuser. The counter is incremented only when the client has had too many errors. Notice how we use short-circuit evaluation to invoke flag_as_abuser only when the too_many_errors rule is true.

```
http-request deny if too_many_errors flag_as_abuser
```

If we want to give a specific client a free pass, so that they won't be denied even if they're getting a lot of error responses, we can whitelist their IP address. Define a whitelist by adding an `acl` that compares the client's source IP, which we can get with the `src` fetch method, against a list of IP addresses or IP ranges. The following would whitelist the IP addresses 10.0.0.5 and 10.0.0.6:

```
acl whitelisted src 10.0.0.5 10.0.0.6
```

We can also whitelist a range of IPs by using CIDR notation:

```
acl whitelisted src 10.0.0.0/24
```

Next, add an `http-request allow` directive before all of your `http-request deny` directives. This will stop HAProxy from processing the deny rules and immediately allow the connection through.

```
http-request allow if whitelisted
```

In addition to specifying the IP addresses inline with the `acl`, we can also specify an external file by using the `src -f` parameter.

```
acl whitelisted src -f /etc/haproxy/whitelist.txt
http-request allow if whitelisted
```

The whitelist.txt file may contain a list of IP address, each on a separate line, as shown:

```
192.168.50.3
192.158.50.4
192.168.50.5
192.168.50.6
```

Note that there shouldn't be any whitespace trailing each IP address. You can also define IP ranges in the file by using CIDR notation:

```
192.168.0.0/16
```

Summary

In this chapter, we discussed how to make your HAProxy load balancer more secure. One way is to run the process in a chroot, which prevents hackers from accessing the entire filesystem should they find a way to inject code into the running HAProxy process. We also discussed how to enable Basic authentication for websites where we'd like to restrict access to only certain users. If we do this, we should make sure that the site is only accessible over HTTPS, since Basic authentication sends credentials over the wire in the clear.

HAProxy gives us ways to defend against several types of attacks including users opening too many connections, users sending very slow HTTP headers or POST bodies, and clients who send many requests or try to download a lot of data within a short amount of time. In addition to stopping these threats, we can also deny attackers for a certain amount of time by flagging them in the `stick-table`. For legitimate users who may trip these alarms, we can add them to a whitelist of trusted IP addresses.

Chapter 12

Command Line

For the most part, you'll likely want to make changes to HAProxy by editing its configuration file and then restarting the service. That way, the changes will be permanent and you can store the file in source control. However, in some cases you will want to update HAProxy's settings dynamically, such as to disable a server before installing software on it or changing a server's weight so that more or less traffic is sent to it.

We can do some of these things by issuing commands directly to the HAProxy process. The changes will be immediate and won't require restarting the service. We can execute these commands by typing them into a command prompt or by storing them in a script to execute later.

In this chapter, we'll cover the following topics:

- Sending commands to the HAProxy socket
- Disabling and enabling servers
- Changing a server's weight
- Viewing and clearing entries in a `stick-table`
- Debugging the HAProxy service

Using socket commands

There are two ways to dynamically interact with HAProxy and both involve sending commands to a Unix domain socket. A socket receives commands and executes them within a program's running process. Sockets were created to allow two processes running on the same machine to send commands to one another, but we can interact with them directly. When HAProxy exposes a socket, we can control it without needing to edit its configuration file or restart its service.

The first way to use a socket is to SSH into the machine and send the commands from there. This makes it easy to restrict who can send commands since it requires an SSH login. It also doesn't require any extra network setup. The second way is to expose the socket over an IP address and port so that you can send commands remotely. This allows us to control HAProxy from another machine, but also means that we must rely on firewall rules to restrict who can access the socket.

Let's discuss using a domain socket from the machine where HAProxy is running first. Start out by updating your /etc/haproxy/haproxy.cfg file so that it has a `stats socket` directive in its `global` section.

```
global
    stats socket /run/haproxy.sock mode 660 level admin
```

The `stats socket` directive adds a Unix domain socket at the path given, in this case /run/haproxy.sock. You can choose any path, but by convention they are often placed within the /run directory. The `mode` parameter restricts the permissions on the socket using standard `chmod` octal digits. A `mode` of 660 grants read and write privileges to the socket's owner and group.

The `level` parameter determines which commands can be used. It can be set to one of the following:

level	meaning
user	Most restrictive. Allows read-only commands that give back non-sensitive information.
operator	All user commands plus some non-risky commands such as `show errors` can be used.
admin	All operator commands plus higher-risk commands such as `disable server` can be used.

After you've added the `stats socket` directive, restart the HAProxy service so that your changes take effect.

```
~$ sudo service haproxy restart
```

Then install a tool called socat. It gives us a way to pipe commands to the socket.

```
~$ sudo apt update
~$ sudo apt install socat
```

Let's try it out with the `show info` command, which returns information about the HAProxy process. We `echo` the command and then pipe it to socat.

```
~$ echo "show info" | sudo socat stdio /run/haproxy.sock
```

You should see something like this:

```
Name: HAProxy
Version: 1.6.9
Release_date: 2016/08/30
Nbproc: 1
Process_num: 1
Pid: 3158
Uptime: 0d 0h29m25s
Uptime_sec: 1765
```

Another useful command is `help`. It returns a list of available commands.

```
~$ echo "help" | sudo socat stdio /run/haproxy.sock
```

Now that we've seen how to send commands from the same machine where HAProxy is, let's move on to learning how to do it remotely. We'll need to expose the socket over an IP address and port. So, add another `stats socket` directive, but this time using the `ipv4@` syntax to specify the IP address of our machine and a high-numbered port of your choosing, like 9999. The VM that I'm using has an IP of 192.168.50.30, so I would add the second `stats socket` directive like so:

CHAPTER 12. COMMAND LINE

```
stats socket /run/haproxy.sock mode 660 level admin
stats socket ipv4@192.168.50.30:9999 level admin
```

On another Linux machine, we can install a tool called netcat, which will allow us to send commands over the network.

```
~$ sudo apt update
~$ sudo apt install netcat
```

On Windows, netcat is included with nmap, available at https://nmap.org. The command is called `ncat` on Windows, but `nc` on Linux. In the following example, we'll use netcat to send the `show info` command to HAProxy from a remote computer. First, `echo` the command and then pipe it to netcat.

```
~$ echo "show info" | nc 192.168.50.30 9999
```

In addition to exposing the Unix domain socket over a specific IP, we can also set an asterisk so that any available IP on the machine can be used.

```
stats socket ipv4@*:9999 level admin
```

We'll cover some other useful commands in the rest of this chapter. More information about HAProxy socket commands can be found at https://cbonte.github.io/haproxy-dconv/1.6/management.html#9.2.

Enabling and disabling a server

Before doing maintenance on a server, you may want to stop the flow of traffic to it. This is what disabling a server in HAProxy does. We could edit the /etc/haproxy/haproxy.cfg file, adding the `disabled` parameter to the `server` directive, as shown:

```
server web1 192.168.50.10:80 check disabled
```

Another option is to disable the server using socket commands, which eliminates the risk of introducing a typo into the configuration. Also, we can send commands remotely. In the following example, we use netcat to disable the web1 server in the webservers `backend`.

```
~$ echo "disable server webservers/web1" | nc 192.168.50.30 9999
```

The `disable server` command is only available if we've set the `stats socket` directive's `level` parameter to admin. This command marks the server as down, stops health checks and immediately routes traffic away from the server. To enable it again, use `enable server`.

```
~$ echo "enable server webservers/web1" | nc 192.168.50.30 9999
```

Another way to disable a server is to put it into maintenance mode by sending the `set server` command with a `state` parameter set to maint. Here's an example:

```
~$ echo "set server webservers/web1 state maint" | nc 192.168.50.30 9999
```

We can also set `state` to drain so that the server is removed from load balancing, but clients with persistent connections will continue to be sent to it. That way they're able to finish out their sessions on it. In drain mode, health checks are not stopped.

```
~$ echo "set server webservers/web1 state drain" | nc 192.168.50.30 9999
```

To enable the server, send a `set server` command with its `state` set to ready.

```
~$ echo "set server webservers/web1 state ready" | nc 192.168.50.30 9999
```

Changing the weight of a server

Recall that we can add a `weight` parameter to a `server` directive to change the proportion of traffic it receives. The amount of traffic it gets is determined by dividing its weight by the sum of all weights. In the following example, web1 will get 4/5 of the traffic and web2 will get 1/5:

```
backend webservers
  balance roundrobin
  server web1 192.168.50.10:80 weight 4
  server web2 192.168.50.11:80 weight 1
```

The downside is that we have to manually edit the configuration file, which makes it harder to include in an automated process. Socket commands give us a way to dynamically change the weight of a server. This comes in handy when we try to implement a strategy like canary deployments wherein we release a new feature to only a small portion of users. With socket commands, we can ratchet a server's weight down remotely, without a service restart. Then when we're satisified with our new feature, we can set the `weight` back to normal.

In the following snippet, we have a `backend` that defines two `server` directives. We've set a `weight` of 50 for both. This will be our starting point, with equal weight assigned to each server.

```
backend webservers
  balance roundrobin
  server web1 192.168.50.10:80 check weight 50
  server web2 192.168.50.11:80 check weight 50
```

I've used 50 so that we'll have wiggle room to adjust the number higher or lower. A server's `weight` can be set to any number between 0 and 256. In the following snippet, we use the `set weight` command to change the webservers/web1 server's weight to 5. This command is only available if we've set the `stats socket` directive's `level` parameter to admin.

```
~$ echo "set weight webservers/web1 5" | nc 192.168.50.30 9999
```

Now, web1 has a weight of 5/55, or 1/11. If you visit the website in your browser, you should only be sent to that server every eleventh time. If you want a user to continue to be sent to the server they started with, add a persistence cookie.

```
backend webservers
  balance roundrobin
  cookie SERVERUSED insert indirect nocache
  server web1 192.168.50.10:80 check weight 50 cookie web1
  server web2 192.168.50.11:80 check weight 50 cookie web2
```

That way, if a client is sent to the new feature group, they'll keep being sent to it for the duration of their session. To see the current weight for a server, use `get weight`.

```
~$ echo "get weight webservers/web1" | nc 192.168.50.30 9999
```

This returns the current and initial weight:

5 (initial 50)

To reset the weight, set it back to 50, like so:

```
~$ echo "set weight webservers/web1 50" | nc 192.168.50.30 9999
```

Working with stick tables

When using a `stick-table` to, for example, track users who have a high rate of errors and subsequently deny their requests, you may want to look inside the table to see which IP addresses have been flagged. First, to get the names of all defined stick tables, use `show table`:

```
~$ echo "show table" | nc 192.168.50.30 9999
```

Here's the result, showing that we have one `stick-table` that's defined in the mywebsite `frontend` section of our configuration file:

    table: mywebsite, type: ip, size:204800, used:1

To show the entries that have been added to that table, append its name to the command, as demonstrated in the following snippet:

```
~$ echo "show table mywebsite" | nc 192.168.50.30 9999
```

CHAPTER 12. COMMAND LINE

Each entry is identified by a unique key that contains the client's IP address. The rest of the entry is comprised of the milliseconds until the entry expires and any associated data types such as the gpc0 counter and http_err_rate, which captures the rate at which the client has received errors:

> table: mywebsite, type: ip, size:204800, used:1 0x21fb000: key=10.0.0.5 use=0 exp=593803 gpc0=1 http_err_rate(5000)=11

We can also check the table repeatedly in a loop. In the next example, we use a while statement that executes the command every half second:

```
~$ while true; do echo "show table mywebsite" |
    nc 192.168.50.30 9999; sleep .5; done
```

Here is the result:

> table: mywebsite, type: ip, size:204800, used:1 0x5560665c5370: key=10.10.0.1 use=0 exp=118377 gpc0=0 http_err_rate(5000)=1
>
> table: mywebsite, type: ip, size:204800, used:1 0x5560665c5370: key=10.10.0.1 use=0 exp=119511 gpc0=0 http_err_rate(5000)=2
>
> table: mywebsite, type: ip, size:204800, used:1 0x5560665c5370: key=10.10.0.1 use=0 exp=119970 gpc0=1 http_err_rate(5000)=17
>
> table: mywebsite, type: ip, size:204800, used:1 0x5560665c5370: key=10.10.0.1 use=0 exp=119993 gpc0=1 http_err_rate(5000)=33

The show table command will return all entries in the stick-table. However, we can filter them based on one of the stored data types by using the data parameter. In the following snippet, we filter our search to only display entries that have a gpc0 counter greater than zero:

```
~$ while true; do echo "show table mywebsite data.gpc0 gt 0" |
    nc 192.168.50.30 9999; sleep .5; done
```

In the following example, we filter the entries to only those that have an HTTP error rate greater than 10:

```
~$ while true; do echo "show table mywebsite data.http_err_rate gt 10" |
    nc 192.168.50.30 9999; sleep .5; done
```

To remove all entries from that table, use the `clear table` command:

```
~$ echo "clear table mywebsite" | nc 192.168.50.30 9999
```

To remove only a specific entry, add the `key` parameter with the IP address of the associated client. In the next example we only remove the entry for IP address 10.0.0.5. If we're denying clients that are flagged in the table, then this person will no longer be denied.

```
~$ echo "clear table mywebsite key 10.0.0.5" | nc 192.168.50.30 9999
```

Debugging the HAProxy service

When logged into the machine where HAProxy is installed, we can get information about the running process by invoking the `haproxy` executable with various arguments. First, whenever we edit the /etc/haproxy/haproxy.cfg file, it'd be nice to verify that we haven't introduced any typos or misconfigurations. To do so, set the -f flag to the path of the configuration file and append the -c flag to check that the file is valid.

```
~$ haproxy -f /etc/haproxy/haproxy.cfg -c
```

The output of this command should be: Configuration file is valid. If there are any errors, they'll be displayed so that we can go in and fix them. It's a good idea to call this command before restarting the HAProxy service, just to make sure things look good.

If you'd like to monitor live traffic that passes through HAProxy, enable debugging with the -d flag. This is safe to do even when the service is already running. Be sure to execut the command as sudo.

```
~$ sudo haproxy -f /etc/haproxy/haproxy.cfg -d
```

We'll get a live feed of requests and responses as they flow through the load balancer. The following snippet shows a request and response being proxied through:

```
GET / HTTP/1.1
Host: 192.168.50.30:81
Connection: keep-alive
Cache-Control: max-age=0
Upgrade-Insecure-Requests: 1
User-Agent: Mozilla/5.0 (Windows NT 10.0; WOW64) AppleWebKit/537.36
  (KHTML, like Gecko) Chrome/51.0.2704.103 Safari/537.36
Accept: text/html,application/xhtml+xml,application/xml;
  q=0.9,image/webp,*/*;q=0.8
Accept-Encoding: gzip, deflate, sdch
Accept-Language: en-US,en;q=0.8
If-None-Match: W/"57781e79-264"
If-Modified-Since: Sat, 02 Jul 2016 20:05:13 GMT

HTTP/1.1 304 Not Modified
Server: nginx/1.9.3 (Ubuntu)
Date: Sat, 02 Jul 2016 20:28:42 GMT
Last-Modified: Sat, 02 Jul 2016 20:05:13 GMT
Connection: keep-alive
ETag: "57781e79-264"
```

When you are finished debugging, type CTRL + C to quit. Note that the service itself will continue running as normal.

Summary

In this chapter, we saw how to dynamically make changes to HAProxy. We can do this after we've SSH'ed into the machine by using the socat program or from a remote computer by using netcat. The key is to set up a Unix domain socket that lets us communicate with the HAProxy process, which we can do with the `stats socket` directive. Using socket commands is faster and more flexible than editing the configuration file directly. It also opens the door to automating our load balancer with scripts or integrating it with our build and deployment tools.

We learned how to disable and enable servers, change a server's weight, and view and clear entries in a `stick-table`. Each can be done on-the-fly without needing to log in and restart the HAProxy service. Last, we saw how to verify that our configuration file is valid and how to debug live traffic, which can be a valuable technique when troubleshooting network-related problems.

Chapter 13

High Availability

HAProxy is great for keeping our websites and other TCP services highly available, but what happens if the load balancer itself breaks down? To prevent it from becoming a single point of failure, we can set up a second load balancer that can take over immediately and automatically when needed. That way, we'll have redundancy not only in case of failure, but also for doing routine maintenance on the machine where HAProxy is running.

We should also think about keeping our HAProxy service highly available between restarts. As we'll see, we can reload the service in a way that prevents dropping any connections. This will be an indispensible technique as we'll likely make many configuration changes over time.

In this chapter, we'll cover the following topics:

- Reloading the HAProxy configuration without dropping connections
- Setting up a failover load balancer
- Replicating data in stick-tables
- Syncing configuration between load balancers

Reloading without a restart

Whenever we make a change to HAProxy's configuration file at /etc/haproxy/haproxy.cfg, we have to reload the service so that it takes effect. Up to this point, we've always done that by executing a hard reset of the service using the `service restart` command like so:

```
~$ sudo service haproxy restart
```

This is quick and easy, but has the major drawback of dropping all active connections from the load balancer. It's like unplugging and plugging back in the power cord. Another drawback is that if your new configuration has an error in it, then when you invoke `service haproxy restart` you'll end up with a stopped service that doesn't restart. An error message like the following will be displayed:

```
Job for haproxy.service failed because the control process exited
  with error code. See "systemctl status haproxy.service" and
  "journalctl -xe" for details.
```

Calling `service haproxy status` will show us that we have an error in our configuration:

```
[ALERT] 260/100616 (3549) : Error(s) found in configuration file
   : /etc/haproxy/haproxy.cfg
[ALERT] 260/100616 (3549) : Fatal errors found in configuration.
haproxy.service: Control process exited, code=exited status=1
Failed to start HAProxy Load Balancer.
haproxy.service: Unit entered failed state.
haproxy.service: Failed with result 'exit-code'.
haproxy.service: Service hold-off time over, scheduling restart.
Stopped HAProxy Load Balancer.
haproxy.service: Start request repeated too quickly.
Failed to start HAProxy Load Balancer.
```

We can invoke `haproxy -f /etc/haproxy/haproxy.cfg -c` to get a description of the error, but your clients won't be able to connect while you're troubleshooting what went wrong. Luckily, there's a command that will update the configuration safely. Use `haproxy reload` to spin up a new HAProxy process that new clients will connect to while clients who are already connected are allowed to finish their requests on the old process. This command will also check whether the configuration file is valid.

CHAPTER 13. HIGH AVAILABILITY

```
~$ /etc/init.d/haproxy reload
```

If there are problems with our new settings, we'll see the following message:

```
[....] Reloading haproxy configuration (via systemctl):
  haproxy.servicehaproxy.service is not active, cannot reload.
 failed!
```

However, checking the service with `service haproxy status` will show that we still have the old process for clients to connect to. If there are no errors and all went well, we'll get a message like this:

```
[ ok ] Reloading haproxy configuration (via systemctl): haproxy.service.
```

Things are looking good, but there's one catch! There's a chance that some new connections could be rejected during the very short time when HAProxy unbinds from the original process to bind the new one. During this time, clients may connect to the old process just before it closes, at which point their connections will be reset. The recommended fix for this is to use the fact that the TCP protocol will retry the connection if we drop it from the very start before it's had a chance to initialize.

The following shell script can be saved as /etc/haproxy/reload_haproxy.sh. It modifies iptables, the Linux firewall, by inserting a rule that drops all new connections to ports 80 and 443 before we try to reload HAProxy. This gives us the freedom to close the old process and bind to the new one, while temporarily putting new requests on hold. The iptables rule is deleted afterwards. From the client's perspective, they'll never know that we briefly stopped accepting new connections because the TCP protocol will keep trying to connect.

```
#! /bin/bash

iptables -I INPUT -p tcp -m multiport --dport 80,443 --syn -j DROP

sleep 1

/etc/init.d/haproxy reload

iptables -D INPUT -p tcp -m multiport --dport 80,443 --syn -j DROP
```

Make the file executable with the following command:

```
~$ sudo chmod u+x /etc/haproxy/reload_haproxy.sh
```

You can now reload your configuration safely by invoking this script from the command line, as shown:

```
~$ sudo /etc/haproxy/reload_haproxy.sh
```

Connections will be reject for a short time, giving HAProxy a change to bind to its new process. Then, connections will be accepted again. Note that you'll need to modify the script if you accept connections over ports other than 80 and 443.

Adding a failover load balancer

HAProxy load balances our backend servers and gives our websites high availability, but what happens when the machine where HAProxy is running fails? To guard against this, we can run two instances of HAProxy at the same time in active-passive mode. If one fails, the other will take over.

We'll use keepalived to accomplish this. Keepalived is a load balancer in its own right, but lacks the features of HAProxy. It does, however, give us a way to create a floating IP, which is an IP address that will bind to whichever machine is up at the moment and has the master role. If the master goes down, the IP will instantly rebind to the backup machine. In this way, we can redirect users to the new load balancer without needing to change DNS to point to a new IP address.

Let's set up two machines running Ubuntu. We'll call the first primary and the second secondary. We'll install keepalived on both. We also want a Web server that's running NGINX. Here is a Vagrantfile that creates the three virtual machines we need:

```
Vagrant.configure(2) do |config|

  config.vm.define "webserver" do |machine|
    machine.vm.box = "gbarbieru/xenial"
    machine.vm.hostname = "webserver"
```

CHAPTER 13. HIGH AVAILABILITY

```
    machine.vm.network "private_network", ip: "192.168.50.32"
  end

  config.vm.define "primary" do |machine|
    machine.vm.box = "gbarbieru/xenial"
    machine.vm.hostname = "primary"
    machine.vm.network "private_network", ip: "192.168.50.30"
  end

  config.vm.define "secondary" do |machine|
    machine.vm.box = "gbarbieru/xenial"
    machine.vm.hostname = "secondary"
    machine.vm.network "private_network", ip: "192.168.50.31"
  end
end
```

Initialize the virtual machines with the **vagrant up** command. Then use **vagrant ssh webserver** to SSH into the webserver machine. The following commands use the apt package manager to install the NGINX webserver on it:

```
~$ sudo apt update
~$ sudo apt install nginx -y
```

Next, **exit** from that machine and **vagrant ssh** into the primary VM. Use apt to install Keepalived and HAProxy there.

```
~$ sudo apt install software-properties-common -y
~$ sudo add-apt-repository ppa:vbernat/haproxy-1.6
~$ sudo apt update
~$ sudo apt install haproxy keepalived -y
```

We can verify that HAProxy and Keepalived were installed by checking their version numbers.

```
~$ haproxy -v
~$ keepalived -v
```

Next, create a file called keepalived.conf in the /etc/keepalived directory. Edit it so that it contains the following configuration:

```
vrrp_instance primary {
  state MASTER
  interface eth1
  virtual_router_id 50
  priority 10
  authentication {
    auth_type PASS
    auth_pass mysecretpassword
  }
  virtual_ipaddress {
    192.168.50.10
  }
}
```

Notice that we are setting our `virtual_ipaddress`, which is our floating IP, to an IP address that hasn't been used yet. Save this file and then restart the keepalived service. Be sure to check its status afterwards with the `service keepalived status` command to make sure things are configured correctly.

```
~$ sudo service keepalived restart
~$ sudo service keepalived status
```

When you check the Keepalived service's status you should see that it has transitioned the VM to the MASTER state. This indicates that this machine currently owns the IP and will serve as the active load balancer.

```
primary Keepalived_vrrp[3036]: Configuration is using : 63328 Bytes
primary Keepalived_vrrp[3036]: Using LinkWatch kernel netlink reflector...
primary Keepalived_healthcheckers[3035]: Initializing ipvs 2.6
primary Keepalived_healthcheckers[3035]: Registering Kernel
  netlink reflector
primary Keepalived_healthcheckers[3035]: Registering Kernel netlink
  command channel
primary Keepalived_healthcheckers[3035]: Opening file
```

CHAPTER 13. HIGH AVAILABILITY

```
'/etc/keepalived/keepalived.conf'.
primary Keepalived_healthcheckers[3035]: Configuration is using : 8188 Bytes
primary Keepalived_healthcheckers[3035]: Using LinkWatch kernel
  netlink reflector...
primary Keepalived_vrrp[3036]: VRRP_Instance(primary)
  Transition to MASTER STATE
primary Keepalived_vrrp[3036]: VRRP_Instance(primary)
  Entering MASTER STATE
```

Now add the following to the end of the /etc/haproxy/haproxy.cfg file so that HAProxy acts as a reverse proxy to our Web server. We will bind to the 192.168.50.10 floating IP, but proxy requests to 192.168.50.32 where our NGINX Web server is listening.

```
listen mywebserver
   bind 192.168.50.10:80 transparent
   balance roundrobin
   server webserver 192.168.50.32:80 check
```

We've added the `transparent` parameter to the `bind` directive. This allows HAProxy to bind to the IP address even if that IP isn't currently bound to this machine. Restart the HAProxy service. Then, do the same on the secondary virtual machine: Install HAProxy and Keepalived, create a file called keepalived.conf in the /etc/keepalived directory, but edit it to contain the following configuration:

```
vrrp_instance secondary {
  state MASTER
  interface eth1
  virtual_router_id 50
  priority 9
  authentication {
    auth_type PASS
    auth_pass mysecretpassword
  }
  virtual_ipaddress {
    192.168.50.10
  }
}
```

This configuration is the same as the one on the primary except that we changed the `vrrp_instance` name and gave it a lower `priority`. A `vrrp_instance` creates a floating IP in our network. The following table sums up the meaning of each setting:

Name	Meaning
state	The machine with the highest priority will become the master, so this doesn't matter. Set it to MASTER.
interface	The network interface to bind the floating IP address to.
virtual_router_id	An arbitrary number between 0 and 255 that should be the same for all machines participating in this cluster.
priority	The order in which machines should assume the role of MASTER if other machines have failed. Those with a larger number come first.
auth_type	How to authenticate. A value of PASS means use a password.
auth_pass	Sets a password for joining the cluster. The password should be the same for all machines.
virtual_ipaddress	The floating IP address to create.

Restart the Keepalived service on the secondary machine and check its status. This time you should see that it has taken the BACKUP role because it has a lower priority:

```
secondary Keepalived_vrrp[3070]: Using LinkWatch kernel
  netlink reflector...
secondary Keepalived_healthcheckers[3069]: Initializing ipvs 2.6
secondary Keepalived_healthcheckers[3069]: Registering Kernel
  netlink reflector
secondary Keepalived_healthcheckers[3069]: Registering Kernel netlink
  command channel
secondary Keepalived_healthcheckers[3069]: Opening file
  '/etc/keepalived/keepalived.conf'.
secondary Keepalived_healthcheckers[3069]: Configuration is using :
  8192 Bytes
secondary Keepalived_healthcheckers[3069]: Using LinkWatch kernel
```

CHAPTER 13. HIGH AVAILABILITY

```
    netlink reflector...
secondary Keepalived_vrrp[3070]: VRRP_Instance(secondary)
    Transition to MASTER STATE
secondary Keepalived_vrrp[3070]: VRRP_Instance(secondary)
    Received higher prio advert
secondary Keepalived_vrrp[3070]: VRRP_Instance(secondary)
    Entering BACKUP STATE
```

Next, update HAProxy's configuration file so that it matches that on the primary. We want the two load balancers to be identical so that when one fails, the other can take over seamlessly. Only one instance of our load balancer will be active at any time.

If you use the `ip addr show` command on the secondary to view the IP addresses that are currently registered on the `eth1` network interface, you should see that 192.168.50.10 is not listed among them.

```
~$ ip addr show eth1
```

However, running the same command on the primary shows that it is listed there:

```
3: eth1: <BROADCAST,MULTICAST,UP,LOWER_UP> mtu 1500 qdisc pfifo_fast
    state UP group default qlen 1000
    link/ether 08:00:27:74:c3:a0 brd ff:ff:ff:ff:ff:ff
    inet 192.168.50.30/24 brd 192.168.50.255 scope global eth1
        valid_lft forever preferred_lft forever
    inet 192.168.50.10/32 scope global eth1
        valid_lft forever preferred_lft forever
```

If you browse to http://192.168.50.10, you should see our website. Here's where things become awesome: If you shut down the primary machine, such as by using the `vagrant halt primary` command, the secondary will get that IP address and our website will continue to be served! If you turn the primary back on with the `vagrant up primary` command, it will take the IP back. You can even see the traffic hitting the primary or the secondary by running a tcpdump packet-capture on either machine:

```
~$ sudo apt update
~$ sudo apt install tcpdump -y
~$ sudo tcpdump -i eth1
```

This will also show you the Virtual Router Redundancy Protocol (VRRP) messages that Keepalived uses to ping each machine to know which are currently up. Use ctrl + C to stop tcpdump.

As a final note, Vagrant always overwrites a VM's IP addresses when `vagrant up` or `vagrant reload` is called. Therefore, it may be necessary to restart the Keepalived service after booting the machine so that the floating IP is reinitialized.

Replicating stick-tables to peers

When we have multiple load balancers for redundancy, we have to think about keeping persistence intact after a failover. Recall that persistence means sending a client to the same backend server for the duration of their session rather than load balancing them among all of our servers. We do this when session data is stored on the backend server, such as data that keeps the user logged in.

If we're using cookies for persistence then there's nothing to worry about. As long as our HAProxy configuration files are identical on the two load balancer machines, then the cookie that's stored in the client's browser will ensure that that person continues to be sent to the `server` that has a matching `cookie` parameter. We really only need to concern ourselves with maintaining persistence when we're using `stick-table` directives.

To that end, HAProxy lets us replicate the `stick-table` data from one machine to another through the use of a `peers` section. A `peers` section identifies all of our HAProxy machines and syncs data between them. This section goes at the same level as a `defaults`, `frontend`, `backend` or `listen`.

If we reuse the Vagrantfile from the Adding a failover load balancer section, our primary load balancer will have an IP address of 192.168.50.30 assigned to it. Our secondary will have an IP of 192.168.50.31. On both machines, modify the /etc/haproxy/haproxy.cfg file so that it has a `peers` section that references these two IP addresses at a high numbered port such as 50000. Also note that we've added a `peers` parameter to the `stick-table` in the mywebserver `listen` section.

```
peers mypeers
    peer primary 192.168.50.30:50000
    peer secondary 192.168.50.31:50000

listen mywebserver
    bind 192.168.50.10:80 transparent
    balance roundrobin
    server webserver 192.168.50.32:80 check
    stick-table type ip size 1m size 1m expire 30m peers mypeers
    stick on src
```

A `peers` section gets a label of your choosing, which I've set to mypeers in this case. Within this section, we add `peer` directives. Each one points to an HAProxy machine. The labels primary and secondary should match the associated machine's hostname. When HAProxy starts up, it finds its own hostname in the list and start listening for data from the others at the given IP and port, such as 192.168.50.30:50000. At the same time, it will use the other `peer` directives and their IP and ports to replicate data out to its peers.

In order to have a `stick-table` participate in replication, we must add a `peers` parameter to it that identifies the `peers` section to use. For example, the following line tells the `stick-table` to join the mypeers group:

```
stick-table type ip size 1m size 1m expire 30m peers mypeers
```

All HAProxy instances in the cluster should have the same `peers` settings. After you've restarted the HAProxy service on each, you can make a request to the website so that an entry is added to the table and then use socket commands to check that the data is replicated. The following command would show you the entries stored in the mywebserver table on the primary:

```
~$ echo "show table mywebserver" | sudo socat stdio /run/haproxy/admin.sock
```

This should show that an entry was added:

```
# table: mywebserver, type: ip, size:1048576, used:1
0x55e053c10544: key=192.168.50.1 use=0 exp=1796618 server_id=1
```

Running this command on the secondary should return the same result. Now, clients will keep their persistence even after a failover because the same data is held on both machines. These benefits extend to other `stick-table` use cases, such as tracking and blocking malicious users.

Syncing configuration

When we have two load balancers, we'll want to keep their configuration files in sync. One way to do this is to use rsync, which is a tool that's available on most Linux distributions and can sync files between two machines. This lets us make changes on one and then invoke rsync to copy them to the other.

Let's reuse the Vagrantfile from earlier in the chapter to spin up three virtual machines: one Web server and a primary and secondary load balancer. After making any change to the /etc/haproxy/haproxy.cfg file on the primary load balancer, use the following rsync command to replicate the change to the secondary machine that's hosted at the IP address 192.168.50.31. Note that I'm using a backslash at the end of the first line so that I can continue the command onto a second line.

```
~$ rsync -avzhe ssh --rsync-path "sudo rsync" \
    /etc/haproxy/haproxy.cfg vagrant@192.168.50.31:/etc/haproxy/
```

Rsync sends the data over an encrypted SSH connection. You will be prompted for the vagrant user's password, which should also be vagrant. Here is the response that you should see letting you know that the data transfer was successful:

```
sending incremental file list

sent 50 bytes   received 12 bytes   24.80 bytes/sec
total size is 1.41K   speedup is 22.81
```

If we create a reload_haproxy.sh script, as described earlier, then we can add this rsync call to the end of it. That way, whenever we update our local configuration and reload the HAProxy service, we'll also be syncing the two machines.

```
#! /bin/bash
```

```
iptables -I INPUT -p tcp -m multiport --dport 80,443 --syn -j DROP

sleep 1

/etc/init.d/haproxy reload

iptables -D INPUT -p tcp -m multiport --dport 80,443 --syn -j DROP

rsync -avzhe ssh --rsync-path "sudo rsync" \
    /etc/haproxy/haproxy.cfg vagrant@192.168.50.31:/etc/haproxy/
```

Rsync will copy the changes we make to the /etc/haproxy/haproxy.cfg file from the primary to the secondary machine, but it won't automatically restart the HAProxy service on the secondary. To fix this, let's update our reload_haproxy.sh script so that it logs into the secondary with SSH and calls **haproxy reload**. Add the following line to the end of the script:

```
ssh vagrant@192.168.50.31 "sudo /etc/init.d/haproxy reload"
```

You will, unfortunately, be asked to enter the user's password twice since we are connecting over SSH again. To fix this, let's switch to using an SSH key instead of a password. Invoke the following command on the primary to generate an SSH key-pair on the primary load balancer:

```
~$ ssh-keygen -t rsa
```

You will be asked where to store the keys and whether you want to add a passphrase. Leave both questions blank and press enter to bypass them. Your keys should now be stored in the ~/.ssh/ directory. The private key will be called id_rsa and the public key will be called id_rsa.pub. We can copy the public key to our secondary load balancer so that when we SSH to it, we'll be allowed to log in without a password because we have the private key on this server.

On the primary machine, use the following command to copy the public key to the secondary server:

```
~$ ssh-copy-id vagrant@192.168.50.31
```

Now we can update our `ssh` command so that it uses the `-i` parameter to specify the location of the id_rsa file.

```
#! /bin/bash

iptables -I INPUT -p tcp -m multiport --dport 80,443 --syn -j DROP

sleep 1

/etc/init.d/haproxy reload

iptables -D INPUT -p tcp -m multiport --dport 80,443 --syn -j DROP

rsync -avzhe "ssh -i /home/vagrant/.ssh/id_rsa" --rsync-path "sudo rsync" \
  /etc/haproxy/haproxy.cfg vagrant@192.168.50.31:/etc/haproxy/

ssh -i /home/vagrant/.ssh/id_rsa vagrant@192.168.50.31 \
  "sudo /etc/init.d/haproxy reload"
```

When you run the script, you should not be asked to enter a password. Here's what it looks like:

```
[ ok ] Reloading haproxy configuration (via systemctl): haproxy.service.
sending incremental file list

sent 50 bytes   received 12 bytes   41.33 bytes/sec
total size is 1.41K   speedup is 22.81
Reloading haproxy configuration (via systemctl): haproxy.service.
```

Our reload script now temporarily stops accepting new connections, reloads HAProxy locally, starts accepting connections again, syncs the configuration to our secondary load balancer by using Rsync and then logs in with SSH and reloads the service on the secondary. All of this happens very quickly when we execute the script.

A good practice is to backup your haproxy.cfg file in a version control system like git. That way, you'll be certain that all of your machines are in sync not only with each other, but also with the file that everyone has access to in git.

Summary

In this chapter, we discussed how to keep our load balancer highly available. We learned that although HAProxy comes with a reload function that tries to reduce downtime between configuration updates, it isn't perfect. By hacking iptables to keep connections queued while we reload the service, we can prevent any requests from being rejected.

We also learned how to set up a backup instance of HAProxy. Using Keepalived, we can use a floating IP to ensure that traffic is routed to the backup immediately after our primary fails. By using `rsync` and `ssh`, we can replicate configuration changes between the servers each time that we reload our service. With these techniques, we can be confident that when our primary load balancer fails, the secondary will be able to take over without problems.

Made in the USA
Lexington, KY
13 April 2017